SPALDING.

Sports Quotes

Joseph Klein

A Division of Howards W. Sams & Company

Published by Masters Press (A Division of Howard W. Sams & Co.)
2647 Waterfront Parkway E. Dr.
Suite 300
Indianapolis, IN 46214

1995 Masters Press

Printed in the United States of America

Library of Congress Cataloging-in-Publication Data
    Klein, Joseph, 1956
    Sports quotes / Joseph Klein.
        p.   cm. -- (Spalding sports library)
    ISBN 1-57028-035-5 (pbk.)
    1. Title. II. Title: Spalding III. Series.
    GV706.8.K54   1995
    796'.0207--dc20   95-4602
                                                                CIP

Credits:
Typography by Leah Marckel
Front Cover Design by Phil Velikan
Proofread by Pat Brady
Editorial assistance provided by Heather Seal

FOREWORD

Well, here it is, *Sports Quotes*, a true labor of love. I have been living with these characters for most of my life, but intensely, for the past four years. It is with feelings of joy and wistfulness, that I offer it to you. My book has finally stopped at this point, but it is never finished for the colorful quotes keep coming on.

A few points about the manuscript. There are many books written about sports, the games, and sports anecdotes. There are a few books of quotations, but they are, for the most part, centered around the individual sports. This is the only book that centers around the players, their dreams, their hurts, their thrills and their agonies.

From rookie to pro, from humble beginnings to outrageous fortunes, from dubious logic to unconventional wisdom, from retirement to growing old...

"Sports is a game called life."

• •

To better understand the situation that prompted each quote, all of the entries are attributed to the individual and his or her position at the time the statement was made.

TABLE OF CONTENTS

Verbal and Cerebral Disconnections

Huh?

Malapropisms, Verbal Confusions, Linguistic Mishaps, Dangling Participles & Double Entendres

All you guys line up alphabetically by height.
> — *Casey Stengel, New York Yankees manager*

Baseball is 90% mental. The other half is physical.
> — *Yogi Berra, New York Yankees catcher*

I don't want to beat a dead horse to death.
> — *Lee Trevino, professional golfer*

You work all your life to get into the Super Bowl. Especially if you're a football player.
> — *Jim McMahon, Chicago Bears quarterback*

I try to tell our guys that the altitude isn't that bad because we're playing indoors.
> — *Jerry Tarkanian, University of Nevada, Las Vegas basketball coach, on playing in Wyoming*

He does a good job of recapping the play before it happens.
> — *Johnny Logan, Milwaukee Braves infielder, on Lou Boudreau, former Cleveland Indians shortstop, turned sportscaster*

I watch a lot of baseball on radio.
> — *Gerald R. Ford, thirty-eighth President of the United States*

We probably won't feel the loss of them until they're gone.

> — *Jerry Tarkanian, UNLV basketball*
> *coach, on graduating players*

I threw about ninety percent fastballs and sliders, fifty percent fastballs, fifty percent sliders—wait, I'm starting to sound like Mickey Rivers.

> — *John Butcher, Texas Rangers pitcher*

From the waist down, Earl Campbell has the biggest legs I've ever seen on a running back.

> — *John Madden, sportscaster*

The runners have returned to their respectable bases.

> — *Dizzy Dean, sportscaster and*
> *former St. Louis Cardinals pitcher*

There's a fly to deep center field. Winfield goes back, back. He hits his head against the wall! It's rolling toward second base!

> — *Jerry Coleman, sportscaster*

If Pete Rose brings the Reds in, they ought to bronze him and put him in cement.

> — *Jerry Coleman, San Diego Padres announcer*

Let's nip this thing in the butt.

> — *Bill Peterson, Florida State football coach*

That ball has a hit in it, so I want it to get back in the ball bag and goof around with the other balls in there. Maybe it'll learn some sense and come out as a pop-up next time.

> — *Mark "The Bird" Fidrych, Detroit Tigers pitcher*

A "flake" is a term created by a right-handed, egotistic, consumeristic, exploitative, non-recycling, carnivorous population. It couldn't have been a term created by a left-hander.

— Bill Lee, Boston Red Sox pitcher

There ain't a left-hander in the world that can run a straight line. It's the gravitational pull on the axis of the earth that gets 'em.

— Ray Miller, Baltimore Orioles coach

Left-handers have more enthusiasm for life. They sleep on the wrong side of the bed and their head gets more stagnant on that side.

— Casey Stengel, New York Mets manager

Except for the teams going under, our league has never been in better shape.

— Gordie Howe, on the state of the World Hockey Association

Reporter: What's the secret to platooning?

Casey Stengel: There's not much to it. You put a right-hand hitter against a left-hand pitcher and a left-hand hitter against a right-hand pitcher and on cloudy days you use a fastball pitcher.

Mickey Mantle can hit just as good right-handed as he can left-handed. He's just naturally amphibious.

— Yogi Berra, New York Yankees catcher

Good pitching will beat good hitting any time, and vice versa.

— Bob Veale, Pittsburgh Pirates pitcher

A good defense always beats a good offense, and vice versa.

— Joe Kuharic, Philadelphia Eagles coach

I've got a great repertoire with my players.

— Danny Ozark, Philadelphia Phillies manager

We're not gonna be any three-clouds-and-a-yard-of-dust kind of team.

— *Bill Peterson, Florida State football coach*

The only thing standing between Jack Perconte and an outstanding major league career is performance.

— *Del Crandall, Seattle Mariners manager*

The sooner you fall behind, the more time you have to catch up.

— *Sam Ogden, writer*

If you can't make the putts and can't get the man in from second in the bottom of the ninth, you're not going to win enough football games in this league, and that's the problem we had today.

— *Sam Rutigliano, Cleveland Browns coach*

Even Napoleon had his Watergate.

— *Danny Ozark, Philadelphia Phillies manager, after the team lost the pennant in the most incredible collapse in the history of major league baseball*

I don't like to look back in retrospect.

— *Vince Ferragamo, Los Angeles Rams quarterback*

Brooks is not a fast man, but his arms and legs move very quickly.

— *Curt Gowdy, sportscaster, on Brooks Robinson, Baltimore Orioles infielder*

Rich Folkers is throwing up in the bullpen.

— *Jerry Coleman, sportscaster*

Thank you ma'am, you don't look so hot yourself.

— *Yogi Berra, New York Yankees catcher, to a female fan who had complimented him on looking cool despite the heat*

I'll never make the mistake of being seventy again.

> — *Casey Stengel, on being fired by*
> *the Yankees for being too old*

Slump? I ain't in no slump. I just ain't hitting.

> — *Yogi Berra, New York Yankees catcher*

To the team captain before a game, "Lead us in a few words of silent prayer".

> — *Bill Peterson, Florida State football coach*

Don't worry about the horse being blind, just load the wagon.

> — *John Madden, Oakland*
> *Raiders coach, to his players*

Sometimes I get lazy and let the dishes stack up. But they don't stack too high. I've only got four dishes.

> — *Mark "The Bird" Fidrych, Detroit Tigers pitcher*

It was hard to have a conversation with anyone, there were so many people talking.

> — *Yogi Berra, New York Yankees*
> *manager, on a White House dinner*

I've seen the future and it's much like the present, only longer.

> — *Dan Quisenberry, Kansas City Royals pitcher*

Better make it four—I don't think I can eat eight.

> — *Yogi Berra, when asked whether he'd*
> *like his pizza cut into four or eight pieces*

My life is a living testimony and is an incongruity and a contradiction to what America has hitherto asked for success.

> — *Don King, fight promoter*

Most people are dead at my age—you could look it up.

> — *Casey Stengel, New York Yankees manager*

My views are just about the same as Casey's.

> — *Mickey Mantle, New York Yankees outfielder,*
> *testifying before a Senate subcommittee who*
> *had just heard incomprehensible testimony*
> *from Casey Stengel*

I'm very appreciative of being indicted.

> — *Bill Peterson, former Florida State University*
> *football coach, on being inducted into the*
> *Florida Hall of Fame*

I'd like to thank all my parents.

> — *Juli Inskter, professional golfer,*
> *on winning a tournament*

Sure, I screwed up that sacrifice bunt, but look at it this way: I'm a better bunter than a billion Chinese.

> — *John Lowenstein, Baltimore Orioles outfielder*

It's really great being Magic Johnson the basketball player for eight months and then just plain Earvin Johnson for the other three.

> — *Magic Johnson, Los Angeles Lakers*

It's so crowded nobody ever goes there anymore.

> — *Yogi Berra, New York Yankees catcher,*
> *on Toots Shor's restaurant*

You know Earl [Weaver], he's not happy unless he's not happy.

> — *Elrod Hendricks, Baltimore Orioles catcher,*
> *quoted by Ron Luciano in* The Umpire
> Strikes Back

I feel better when I'm sick.

> — *Roberto Clemente, Pittsburgh Pirates*
> *outfielder, on being a hypochondriac*

Those guys couldn't understand the language I was pitching them in. That's why I struck out so many.

> — *Vinegar Bend Mizell, St. Louis Cardinals*
> *pitcher, on pitching in Cuba*

How do I know? I'm not in shape yet.

> — *Yogi Berra, New York Yankees catcher,*
> *when asked his hat size*

If it wasn't for golf, I'd probably be a caddie today.

> — *George Archer, professional golfer*

Don't fail to miss tomorrow's game.

> — *Dizzy Dean, St. Louis Cardinals announcer*

That's no hair off my chest.

> — *Martina Navratilova, professional tennis player*

I only know how to play two ways: reckless and abandon.

> — *Magic Johnson, Los Angeles Lakers*

I'm not afraid of Jack [Nicklaus]. If you play better than he does, you can beat him.

> — *Tom Weiskopf, professional golfer*

How did they get my picture? I've never been to New York.

> — *Sam Snead, professional golfer, on*
> *seeing his picture in the New York Times*

If I wasn't talking, I wouldn't know what to say.

> — *Chico Resch, New York Islanders goalie*

All we have to do is capitalize on our mistakes.

> — *Bill Peterson, Florida State football coach*

They should move first base back a step to eliminate all the close plays.

> — *John Lowenstein, Baltimore Orioles outfielder*

It didn't do any good. My neck still hurts.

> — *Ira Gordon, Tampa Bay Buccaneers guard,*
> *after receiving a neck x-ray.*

What do you think I am, a geologist?

> — *Bill Peterson, Florida State football coach,*
> *when asked if he thought it would rain*

There is one word in America that says it all, and that one word is, 'You never know.'

> — *Joaquin Andujar, St. Louis Cardinals pitcher*

We keep beating ourselves, but we're getting better at it.

> — *Hank Bullough, Buffalo Bills football coach*

I don't think either team is capable of winning.

> — *Warren Brown, sportswriter, on the World Series*
> *between the Detroit Tigers and the Chicago*
> *Cubs in 1945*

He has a lot of inept ability.

> — *Hank Bullough, Buffalo Bills head coach*

Reporter: Yogi, have you made up your mind whether to take the job as Mets' manager?

Yogi Berra: Not that I know of.

Secretariat is only human.

> — *Steve Pinkus, agent*

I can't tell you exactly what I intend to do, but I can tell you one thing, it won't be anything rational.

> — *Calvin Griffith, Minnesota Twins owner,*
> *on hiring a new manager*

It could permanently hurt a batter for a long time.

> — *Pete Rose, Cincinnati Reds player-manager,*
> *on the brushback pitch*

The doctors X-rayed my head and found nothing.

> — *Dizzy Dean, St. Louis Cardinals pitcher*

If I drop dead tomorrow, at least I'll know I died in good health.

> — *Bum Phillips, Houston Oilers coach,*
> *after he was pronounced fit after a medical exam*

I think the lay-off was the greatest thing to happen to Baylor football. I'll figure out why later.

> — *Grant Teaff, Baylor football coach,*
> *after a 3-week lay-off*

My sister's expecting a baby and I don't know if I'm going to be an uncle or an aunt.

> — *Chuck Nevitt, N.C. State basketball star,*
> *on why he has been nervous recently*

Today is Father's Day. So everyone out there, Happy Birthday.

> — *Ralph Kiner, NY Mets announcer*

It's almost like we have ESPN.

> — *Magic Johnson, Los Angeles Lakers,*
> *on how he and James Worthy team up so well*

Well, hi everybody, and welcome to New York Yankee baseball. I'm Bill White.

— Phil Rizzuto, NY Yankee announcer

He once asked a waitress to put some "neutrons" on his salad.

— George F. Will, Newsweek, on pitcher Mike Smith

I still have it. I just keep it shaved.

— Gary Gaetti, Minnesota Twins, on his moustache

I've been traveling so much, I haven't had time to grow it.

— Bob Horner, Atlanta Braves, why he no longer sports a beard

I've never had major knee surgery on any other part of my body.

— Winston Bennett, Kentucky basketball star, after knee surgery

Just remember the words of Henry Patrick: "Kill me or let me live."

— Bill Peterson, Florida State football coach, on trying to motivate his players

I used to have the worst time remembering names. Then I took the Sam Carnegie course and I've been all right ever since.

— Bill Callahan, University of Missouri, sports public relations director

Some of the great Oedipuses in the world have been built by Donald Trump.

— Don King, boxing promoter

I don't know if I am as fast as I was, but I don't think I'm any slower.

> — *Floyd Patterson, ex-heavyweight champ*

I suffer from acrophobia. I can't look out of high buildings. I don't even like to ride in planes. I guess that's what makes me a good sky diver.

> — *Jeanni McCombs, top U.S. skydiver*

We'll jump off that bridge when we come to it.

> — *Matt Goukas, Philadelphia 76ers coach,*
> *on when he planned to use a player*

That was the nail that broke the coffin's back.

> — *Jack Kraft, Villanova basketball coach,*
> *after his star player fouled out*

Well, that's football.

> — *Ray Fosse, Cleveland Indians catcher,*
> *after a collision at home plate*

I want to thank the university for what it's done to me the past four years.

> — *Roger Perrix, University of Cincinnati football guard*

I called the doctor and he told me that the contraptions were an hour apart.

> — *Mackey Sasser, New York Mets catcher,*
> *when his wife was giving birth*

There's a lot of heredity in that family.

> — *Ralph Kiner, New York Mets announcer,*
> *on Steve Trout, New York Yankees pitcher,*
> *whose father, Dizzy, also pitched in the majors*

Please let people know that, off the record, I'm very quotable.

> — *Terry Donahue, UCLA football coach*

I'm exuberated. I think that's a word.

> — *Phil Frasch, San Jose State quarterback,*
> *after beating Stanford*

Wes Parker was originally born in Chicago.

> — *Curt Gowdy, TV announcer*

We gave the interior decorator an unlimited budget and he exceeded it.

> — *Lamar Hunt, Kansas City Chiefs football*
> *owner, on his new fancy office*

I must have had ambrosia.

> — *Jim Ganter, Milwaukee Brewers, on not showing up for*
> *a radio show*

I took a hunting trip to one of those Canadian proverbs.

> — *Jim Ganter, Milwaukee Brewers, about a trip*

The trouble with officials, they just don't care who wins.

> — *Tommy Canterbury, Centenary basketball coach*

It's good to have a guy running in my district that I don't have to worry about.

> — *Rep. Joseph Moakley, Boston, on Boston Marathon*
> *winner Bill Rodgers*

They've got the same people as last year, but not the same players.

> — *Tom McVie, Winnipeg Jets coach, on the Buffalo*
> *Sabres, who are playing better than last year*

I don't care what religion he is. If he doesn't get moving, he's gonna lose this fight.

> — *Gil Clancy, announcer for Davis-Hernandez lightweight*
> *bout, on hearing that Davis was a vegetarian*

Strength is my biggest weakness.

> — *Mark Snow, New Mexico basketball player,*
> *a very slim 6'10", on his talents*

We reviewed our ethnic composition of our student body and found we were unbalanced. We needed a quarterback.

> — *Al Cementina, Lick High School football coach, after*
> *Jim Plunkett transferred to his school*

I thought they said steak dinner, but then I found it was a State dinner.

> — *Yogi Berra, at a dinner at the White House*

You can observe a lot by watching.

> — *Yogi Berra*

I'm going to cancel my prescription.

> — *Bob Stanley, Boston Red Sox,*
> *after being blasted by a local paper*

I'm going to graduate on time, no matter how long it takes.

> — *Rod Brooken, University of Michigan basketball player*

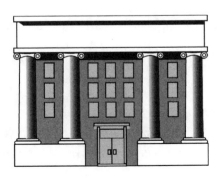

DUMB REMARKS

Dumb Questions & Answers to Dumb Questions

That's why I hate to play good.

> — *Darryl Dawkins, New Jersey Nets, after scoring a career high, 36 points, and being mobbed by the press*

I told him we needed an ultrasound machine and he asked me why we needed music in the locker room.

> — *Lennie Wilkens, Seattle SuperSonics coach, roasting general manager Zollie Volchok*

I don't know. I don't see her that much.

> — *Ray Perkins, Tampa Bay Buccaneers coach, on whether his wife complains about his long work days*

Naw, I didn't die last night. I wasn't even out of the house.

> — *Willie Pep, former heavyweight champion, on a rumor that he had died*

I bet he couldn't make that play again, not even on instant replay.

> — *Red Schoendienst, St. Louis Cardinals, referring to a sensational catch by Roberto Clemente*

The sky is so clear today you can see all the way to Missouri.

> — *Jerry Coleman, announcer, broadcasting a game in Kansas City*

It puzzles me how they know what corners are good for filling stations. Just how did these fellows know where there was gas and oil under there.

> — *Dizzy Dean, pitcher, when he drove into a gas station*

I..., I..., I couldn't have done it without my bowling ball.

> *— Millie Ignizio, female bowler, on what she*
> *attributed her better than 200 average*

That'll be the 28th penalty of the game. It's the 14th against Washington and either the 13th or 14th against New York. I don't know which.

> *— ESPN*

What's a decade?

> *— Muhammad Ali, heavyweight champion,*
> *on being named Athlete of the Decade*

Sure I've got one. It's a perfect 20-20.

> *— Duane Thomas, Dallas Cowboys,*
> *when asked about his IQ*

Are you any relation to your brother, Marv?

> *— Leon Wood, NY Jets, to team announcer Steve Albert*

The game will start at 5 p.m. Pacific Coast League Daylight time.

> *— Ralph Kiner, NY Mets announcer*

Did they think I might go somewhere else?

> *— Jim Sweeny, Washington State football coach, after a*
> *losing season, the regents tore up his one year contract*
> *and gave him a new three year contract*

It's not politics. It's just who you know.

> *— Paul Guanzon, sports announcer, on how one*
> *becomes a sports announcer*

You drive the car, you don't carry it.

> *— Janet Guthrie, racing car driver, on strength*

We are very proud. He's our first offensive lineman to ever become President.

> — *Will Perry, Michigan sports publicist,*
> *on ex-Wolverine, Gerald Ford*

One of the advantages bowling has over golf is that you seldom lose a bowling ball.

> — *Don Carter, bowling pro*

The singin's easy. Memorizin' the words is hard.

> — *Rocky Graziano, former middleweight*
> *champion, on his singing career*

It was after he hit it.

> — *Tommy John, NY Yankees pitcher, after George Bell's*
> *long home run, when asked if the pitch was out of the*
> *strike zone*

How could it be mental? I don't have a college education.

> — *Steve Farr, Kansas City Royals pitcher,*
> *that his sore shoulder could be mental*

This is a good story. Usually they just take your biology and rewrite it.

> — *Harry Coyle, NBC baseball director*

There comes a time in every man's life and I've had plenty of them.

> — *Casey Stengel*

INTELLIGENCE

Brains of Brawns

He's got an IQ of about room temperature.

> — Dan Hampton, Chicago Bears defensive end, describing
> Mark Gastineau

I think our players are excited about the prospect of playing Arizona State, but that might not speak a lot for their intelligence.

> — Bob Cope, Pacific football coach, when
> facing heavily-favored Arizona State

I told Lew Alcindor we wouldn't accept him until he took back what he said about the University of Wisconsin. What he said was, "I won't come."

> — John Erickson, Wisconsin basketball coach,
> on trying to recruit Alcindor

We've learned our lesson. We won't recruit anybody that's intelligent again.

> — Duffy Daugherty, Michigan State football coach,
> when a star player with a 3.99 average quit the
> team to enter medical school

He doesn't know the meaning of the word "fear." Of course, there are lots of other words he doesn't know either.

> — Sid Gilman, San Diego Chargers coach,
> on one of his first year players

Even football players know they're in trouble when the propellers don't go around.

> — Tom Harp, Indiana State football coach,
> after his team made a forced landing

I don't understand the questions of things he can answer.

> — *Ed Lynch, New York Mets, on teammate and Yale graduate, Ron Darling*

Everybody wants to see Oscar Robertson...that's everybody except me.

> — *Dudley Moore, Duquense University basketball coach, when his team had to play against the star*

Patience is our biggest problem.

> — *Grant Teaff, Baylor football coach, on Baylor's not winning a Southwest Conference title since 1924*

He's one of the smartest guys to put on sneakers, since Einstein.

> — *Stan Morrison, USC basketball coach, on an opposing player*

You've got guys from MIT and guys who can't spell MIT.

> — *Sylvester Stallone, on the wide range of interest in arm wrestling*

FAMOUS LAST WORDS

Ruth made a great mistake when he gave up pitching. Working once a week, he might have lasted a long time and become a great star.

> — *Tris Speaker, Cleveland Indians manager,*
> *on Babe Ruth*

You've bought yourself a cripple.

> — *Bill Terry, NY Giants manager, to Yankee executive*
> *George Weiss, on the Yankees' signing Joe DiMaggio*

Don't do it...I've seen a sandlot team clobber him. All he'll do is take up space for two years and give the papers more ammunition to throw at you.

> — *Branch Rickey, Jr., Brooklyn Dodger executive, advising*
> *his father not to sign Sandy Koufax*

The kid can't play baseball. He can't pull the ball.

> — *Tommy Holmes, minor league manager,*
> *on Hank Aaron*

Just so-so in center field.

> — *New York Daily News review of Willie Mays' debut*

He won't make it.

> — *Gordon Goldsberry, Chicago Cubs scout,*
> *on Tom Seaver*

He'll never be more than a 13 or 14 game winner. He's a momma's boy.

> — *Johnny Sain, Chisox pitching coach, on Tommy John*

If Stanford wins a single game with that crazy formation, you can throw all the football I ever knew into the Pacific Ocean.

> *— Pop Warner, on the T formation*

Just a fad—a passing fancy.

> *— Phillip Wrigley, Chicago Cubs owner, on night baseball*

I'll never quit. When I do leave, I'll die on the 50-yard line at Ohio stadium, in front of 87,000 people.

> *— Woody Hayes, Ohio State football coach*

We plan absentee ownership. I'll stick to building ships.

> *— George Steinbrenner, NY Yankees owner,*
> *when he bought the team*

Bob Lemon is going to be our manager all year. You can bet on it. I don't care if we come in last. I swear on my heart he'll be the manager all season.

> *— George Steinbrenner, New York Yankees owner,*
> *who then fired Lemon in mid-April*

Kid, you're too small. You ought to go out and shine shoes.

> *— Casey Stengel, New York Yankees manager,*
> *to Phil Rizzuto*

Playing the Russians will be a lesson in futility. You know what our chances are? Slim and none.

> *— Herb Brooks, U.S. Olympic hockey coach,*
> *just before his team defeated the Russians*

This time, Leonard will kiss the floor of the ring because he talks too much.

> *— Roberto Duran, before losing his second fight*
> *to Sugar Ray Leonard*

Willie Mays seems to be swinging bad.

> *— Warren Spahn, Milwaukee Braves pitcher, just*
> *before Mays hit four home runs in one game*

LET'S TALK

I have an off-season vocabulary, and a during-season vocabulary.
> — *Elliott Maddox, NY Mets, saying*
> *that he was bilingual*

He has only two speeches, the short one, "Thank you," and the long one, "Thank you very much." I like the long one.
> — *Mrs. Phil K. Wrigley, wife of the*
> *quiet Chicago Cubs owner*

My wife, Beth, and I have a little trouble communicating. When I say "a broad" she thinks about a trip to Europe. When she says "diamond" I think of baseball.
> — *Lou Holtz, Notre Dame coach*

I was thinking of a slow motion replay. On second thought I decided it would be redundant.
> — *Roone Arledge, after Willie McCovey,*
> *Giants, stole second*

This is my sixth year with the Bears. Jim McMahon has been with the Bears six years, too, and people say we don't communicate. That's not true. We've talked four times.
> — *Mike Ditka, Chicago Bears coach*

He only needs one..."Give me the ball."
> — *Magic Johnson, Los Angeles Lakers, after he heard that*
> *Akeem Olajuwon speaks six languages*

I don't say it. I think it.
> — *Billy Graham, evangelist, when he misses a putt*

I kept feeling like the Hindu snake charmer with a deaf cobra.

> — *Bill Fitch, Houston Rockets basketball coach, on poor communication with his team*

I yelled from the dugout, "Watch the squeeze," and then I watched it.

> — *Earl Weaver, Baltimore Orioles manager, on the opposition pulling a suicide squeeze play*

I'll always remember his pep talks. One time there were only 72 bleeps in it, and that was Christmas Day.

> — *Paul Westphal, commenting on the 'language' used by Boston Celtic coach Tom Heinsohn*

It's the first role I've played in a foreign language.

> — *Charles Durning, actor, playing the part of Casey Stengel on Broadway*

Excuse me, Casey, now I have to throw this upstairs to our translators.

> — *Tony Kubek, NBC, after talking with Casey Stengel*

I cussed him out in Spanish, and he threw me out in English.

> — *Lou Piniella, NY Yankees outfielder, after being thrown out of a game by Armando Rodriquez*

Like the time, I ask my caddie for a sand wedge and he comes back 10 minutes later with a ham on rye.

> — *Chi Chi Rodriguez, golf pro, on his accent*

I talked to the ball in Spanish, but I found out it was an American ball.

> — *Mike Cuellar, Cuban-born Baltimore Orioles pitcher*

I want little conversation and lots of hair on the floor.

> — *Bum Phillips, New Orleans Saints coach, to his barber*

PLAY ON WORDS

Clichés, Puns & Wise Cracks

And so they escorted her off the field, two a breast.

> — Si Burick, Dayton Daily News sports editor, writing
> about Morganna, the well-endowed dancer, being
> taken from a baseball field by four guards

If I'm a left-handed John Elway, I'm underpaid and underpublicized. I would say that he's a right-handed Boomer Esiason, but that would mean he would be overpaid and overpublicized.

> — Boomer Esiason, Cincinnati Bengals quarterback, when
> asked if he were a left-handed John Elway

I used to play the violin when I was younger, but one day I broke the strings and I just didn't have the guts to play.

> — Duffy Daugherty, Michigan State football coach,
> on his musical background

Every horse I've had is wide awake and slow as hell.

> — John Gavers, horse trainer, if he had any
> sleepers that might win

It's a snap.

> — Butch Adler, Purdue, how it felt switching
> from linebacker to center

We call him Don Juan. The girls Don Juan him.

> — Bob Henko, Tampa Bay Buccaneers, on Chris
> Collinsworth, making fun of his playboy image

Well, we don't take a boy unless we need him.

> — *Duffy Daugherty, Michigan State football coach, on how "need" is determined in deciding scholarships*

Which is going to come first for Bob Knight, cardiac arrest, or just arrest?

> — *Todd Phipers, Denver Post writer*

I don't know. I never felt his nose.

> — *Gordie Howe, Detroit Red Wings hockey star, when asked if he thought a player was a "hard-nosed player"*

That's right Harry. I went to bed with a lot of old bats in my day.

> — *Richie Ashburn, retired baseball player, explaining the good care he took of his baseball bats*

You talk about Rhodes scholars. I was asked to hit the Rhode twice when I was at Stanford.

> — *John Brodie, football star*

He may be a late starter, but he's an early finisher.

> — *Bob Ussery, on the horse, Reflected Glory*

I was just trying to give the league a little exposure.

> — *Paul Cannell, Washington Diplomats soccer team, on being suspended for dropping his pants at a game*

He kicks them so high and so short you can't run them back. You have to fair catch everyone. Us coaches call that the punt of no return.

> — *Ernal Allen, Dallas Cowboys coach, on kicker Bill Bradley*

There are the pros and cons of track.

> — *Brian Oldfield, shotputter, on professional track stars who are paid and amateurs who take money under the table*

I t's not often we get to see The Lone Ranger and Toronto on the same night.

> — *Bobby Bragan, Texas Rangers, after Clayton Moore (The Lone Ranger) made an appearance at a game with Toronto*

N o, I dream about girls.

> — *Dextor Clinkscale, Dallas Cowboys, whether he dreamed that the Cowboys would ever give up 50 points in a game*

W hat's that, a baggie?

> — *Jacob Green, Seattle Seahawks, on the statistic, "half-sack"*

S horts.

> — *Chuck Doyle, Holy Cross, on what he runs the 40 yard dash in*

A bout 6 or 7. Spanish, Argentine, Cuban, Mexican...

> — *Severiano Ballesteros, golf pro, from Spain, on how many languages he speaks*

I don't know what he was complaining about. The club does their dry cleaning.

> — *Billy Gardner, Minnesota Twins manager, fined $150 for spitting tobacco juice on an umpire*

W ell, if I didn't, it would fall over.

> — *John Brodie, San Franciscon 49ers, on why a high salary player had to hold the ball for field goals and extra points*

I n Los Angeles or San Francisco. I forgot which.

> — *Danny Murtaugh, Pittsburgh Pirates manager, in answer to where he thought his team would finish*

It will seat six fisherman or 12 lovers.

> — *Jack Nicklaus, golf pro, on the seating capacity of his yacht*

His contract.

> — *Jerry Rhone, Los Angeles Raiders quarterback, on what he liked about Jim Plunkett*

Probably the Beatles' white album.

> — *Steve Largent, Seattle Seahawks, on which record he will cherish the most*

That's the only hope he's got.

> — *Muhammad Ali, when asked if Chuck Wepner was a great white hope*

You asked if he can play for the Clippers and if he can play in the NBA. That's two different questions.

> — *Pete Babcock, San Diego Clippers, on a draft choice*

I don't know. I never hit myself.

> — *Elisha Obed, boxer, on his best punch*

Rapport? You mean like, "You run as fast as you can and I'll throw as far as I can"?

> — *Jeff Kemp, San Francisco 49ers quarterback, on his rapport with Jerry Rice*

Maybe I'll make the simulated All-Star team.

> — *Barry Lyons, NY Mets back-up catcher, after he went six for six in a simulated game against Tom Seaver*

W ISE CRACKS

I was recruited by Sid Gillman. I was coached by Woody Hayes and Ara Parseghian, and I coached with Bo Schembechler. At Indiana, I was closely associated with Bobby Knight. All of these quiet, reserved, unemotional individuals left their marks on me.

> — *John Pont, now in insurance*

W hy should I feel sorry for Ali? He got 2.5 million dollars for being beaten up. Most of us in this city have to pay for the privilege.

> — *Fight fan, New York City*

I 'm especially grateful to Coach Dickey for giving me so much time to study during games.

> — *Thom Clifford, Florida reserve running back, after receiving an award for highest academic achievement*

W hen did you first know you had a no-hitter?

> — *Anonymous sportswriter to Billy Conn, heavyweight contender, after his defeat by Joe Louis*

T hank God! They electrocuted the chef.

> — *Jimmy Cannon, sportswriter, when the lights flickered during a baseball writers' dinner*

I play in the low 80s. If it's any hotter than that, I won't play.

> — *Joe E. Lewis, comedian*

M ike Anderson's limitations are limitless.

> — *Danny Ozark, Philadelphia Phillies manager*

Once we went out to eat and he picked up the check.

> — *M.L. Carr, Boston Celtics forward, on teammate*
> *Larry Bird's most amazing feat*

There are only two places in this league: first place and no place.

> — *Tom Seaver, New York Mets pitcher*

People always ask me if success is going to change me, and I tell them I sure hope so.

> — *Randall "Tex" Cobb, heavyweight boxer*

Dale's going to go out and paint the town beige.

> — *Ernie Johnson, Atlanta Braves announcer, on*
> *clean-living Dale Murphy's being named*
> *National League MVP*

We start seven naturalized citizens. They are as American as Henry Kissinger.

> — *Menahem Less, Adelphi College soccer coach,*
> *responding to charges that his team relied too*
> *heavily on foreign players*

I fought Sugar Ray so many times it's a wonder I didn't get diabetes.

> — *Jake LaMotta, former middleweight champion*

An hour later we wanted to play them again.

> — *Rocky Bridges, minor league manager, recalling*
> *a game against a Chinese team*

He can run, but he can't hide.

> — *Joe Louis, former heavyweight champion, on his*
> *upcoming fight with Billy Conn*

Musically speaking, if Holmes don't C-sharp, he'll B-flat.

> — *Muhammad Ali, heavyweight champion, on an*
> *upcoming bout with Larry Holmes*

Jeez, it wasn't that good a game.

> — *Dick Young, sportswriter, to a man who had*
> *a heart attack during the All-Star game*

It's not whether you win or lose, but who gets the blame.

> — *Blaine Nye, Dallas Cowboys lineman*

You've gone from a human vacuum cleaner to a litterbug.

> — *Dave McNally, Baltimore Orioles pitcher,*
> *to teammate Brooks Robinson after Robinson*
> *made three errors in nine games*

Hearing the crowd was great. It made what little hair I have stand on end.

> — *Alex English, Denver Nuggets forward,*
> *on receiving a standing ovation*

Things were so bad in Chicago last summer that by the fifth inning they were selling hot dogs to go.

> — *Ken Brett, California Angels pitcher*

I slept like a baby. Every two hours I woke up and started crying.

> — *Tom McVie, New Jersey Devils coach,*
> *after a tough loss*

I think it would be a good idea.

> — *John McKay, Tampa Bay Buccaneers coach, asked about*
> *his team's execution after a loss*

They do one-arm push-ups so they can count with the other hand.

> — *Al McGuire, former Marquette University basketball*
> *coach, on football players*

It certainly was a great thrill. And someday he can tell his grandchildren that he hit against me.

> — *Doc Medich, Pittsburgh Pirates pitcher, on*
> *pitching to Hank Aaron*

The only difference between me and General Custer is that I have to watch the films on Sunday.

> — *Rick Venturi, Northwestern University football coach*

I haven't read it yet.

> — *Johnny Unitas, Baltimore Colts quarterback,*
> *when asked about his new book*

Because of us, there's the no clothesline rule, the no-spearing rule, the no-hitting-out-of-bounds rule, the no-fumbling-forward-in-the-last-two-minutes-of-the-game rule, the no-throwing-helmets rule and the no Stickum rule. So you see, we're not all bad.

> — *Ted Hendricks, Los Angeles Raiders linebacker*

If it's my wife, tell her I'm not here.

> — *Joe Forte, NCAA basketball official, to reporters,*
> *as a phone rang while he was running past*
> *the press table during a game*

What are you trying to do, take my fans away from me?

> — *Marv Throneberry, New York Mets infielder, when*
> *teammate Frank Thomas made two errors on one*
> *play*

When the list of great coaches is finally read, I believe Layden will be there listening.

> — *Pat Williams, Philadelphia 76ers general manager,*
> *on Utah Jazz coach Frank Layden*

We've got a problem here. Luis Tiant wants to use the bathroom, and it says no foreign objects in the toilet.

> — *Graig Nettles, New York Yankees infielder*

They've played on grass and they've played on AstroTurf. What they should do is put down a layer of paper in Candlestick Park. After all, the Giants always look good on paper.

> — *Don Rose, disk jockey, on the San Francisco Giants*

Any time your defense gives up more points than the basketball team, you're in trouble.

> — *Lou Holtz, University of Minnesota football coach*

The Houston Astros play in a vast indoor stadium known as the Astrodome, but the problem is they field a half-vast team.

> — *Kurt Bevacqua, San Diego Padres infielder*

Through years of experience I have found that air offers less resistance than dirt.

> — *Jack Nicklaus, professional golfer, on why*
> *he tees up his ball so high*

You mean I got traded for Dooley Womack? The Dooley Womack?

> — *Jim Bouton, New York Yankees pitcher*

He can eat apples off a tree without using his hands.

> — *Norm Van Brocklin, Philadelphia Eagles coach,*
> *on 6'8" receiver Harold Carmichael*

I lost it in the sun.

> — *Billy Loes, Brooklyn Dodgers pitcher,*
> *on why he booted a grounder*

I can't play perfect every day.

> — *Teddy Martinez, New York Mets infielder,*
> *after making five errors in five games*

I wasn't aware I had a perfect night.

> — *Dennis Awtry, Phoenix Suns guard, on*
> *learning he'd gone 0 for 7 from the field*

It's not a foreign substance. It's made right here in the United States.

> — *Al Braverman, fight manager, in response to the charge*
> *that he adminstered a foreign substance to his fighter*

The Washington Senators and the New York Giants must have played a doubleheader this afternoon—the game I saw and the game Graham McNamee announced.

> — *Ring Lardner, sportswriter*

We like our receivers to have both [speed and quickness], but if they had both, they'd be at USC.

> — *Lavell Edwards, Brigham Young*
> *University football coach*

He's turned his life around. He used to be depressed and miserable. Now he's miserable and depressed.

> — *Harry Kalas, Philadelphia Phillies announcer,*
> *on Phillies outfielder Gary Maddox*

He might have found Jesus, but he's having a terrible time finding Moses.

> — *Morris Siegel, sportswriter, on Denver Broncos*
> *born- again quarterback Craig Morton's inability*
> *to hit receiver Haven Moses.*

I'm glad we're not going to the Gator Bowl.

> — *Lou Holtz, University of Arkansas football coach,*
> *after being bombarded with oranges by fans*

I was on the dance floor, but I couldn't hear the band.

> — *Chi Chi Rodriguez, professional golfer, on a long putt*

He floats like an anchor, stings like a moth.

> — *Ray Gandolf, sports commentator,*
> *on 39-year-old Muhammad Ali*

If Bud Grant and Tom Landry were in a personality contest, it would be a 0-0 tie.

> — *Don Meredith, sportscaster and former*
> *Dallas Cowboys quarterback*

Having Marv Throneberry play for your team is like having Willie Sutton play for your bank.

> — *Jimmy Breslin, writer*

They should put a sign on the 10-yard line saying, THE BUCS STOP HERE.

> — *Jack Harris, sportscaster, on the*
> *Tampa Bay Buccaneers*

The film looks suspiciously like the game itself.

> — *Bum Phillips, New Orleans Saints coach,*
> *viewing the films of a one-sided loss*

I've already told prospective customers that after I open the store, when anybody buys a sofa, I'll throw in a chair.

> — *Bobby Knight, Indiana University basketball coach,*
> *on rumors that he plans to open a furniture store*

We're on a first-number basis. He calls me three, and I call him two.

> — *Bill Lee, Boston Red Sox pitcher (number 37), on Mark*
> *"The Bird" Fidrych, Detroit Tigers pitcher (number 20)*

I've got a jackass back in Oklahoma, and you can work him from sunup till sundown and he ain't never going to win the Kentucky Derby.

> — *Pepper Martin, St. Louis Cardinals outfielder,*
> *on the futility of two-a-day workouts*

I found a delivery in my flaw.

> — *Dan Quisenberry, Kansas City Royals relief pitcher,*
> *diagnosing his pitching problems*

If they want somebody to play third base, they got me. If they want somebody to attend luncheons, they should hire George Jessel.

> — *Graig Nettles, New York Yankees infielder*

He hasn't much range, but anything he can get to, he'll drop.

> — *Red Smith, sportswriter, on Harmon Killebrew,*
> *Minnesota Twins infielder*

They had the distinction of disgracing themselves from coast to coast instead of just locally.

> — *William Clay Ford, Detroit Lions owner,*
> *on his team's loss on network television*

No, I clean giraffe ears.

> — *Elvin Hayes, NBA star, asked if*
> *he was a basketball player*

All those who need showers, take them.

> — *John McKay, University of Southern California football*
> *coach, to his players after a one-sided loss*

I don't expect to win enough games to be put on NCAA probation. I just want to win enough to warrant an investigation.

> — *Bob Devaney, University of Nebraska football coach*

If you can't stand the heat, stay out of The Chicken.

> — *Ted Ginnoulas, The San Diego Chicken,*
> *on wearing the costume during a heat wave*

George Chuvalo's best punch is a left cheek to the right glove.

> — *Larry Merchant, sportswriter*

Hallacy is the boxer in the green trunks and the red blood.

> — *Don Dunphy, ring announcer*

If I'm lucky, in five or six years I'll be the one being booed.

> — *Steve Bono, Minnesota Vikings reserve*
> *quarterback, on becoming a starter*

If horse racing is the sport of kings, then drag racing must be the sport of queens.

> — *Bert R. Sugar, sportswriter*

I don't care what you say. I think Kent Benson has a future in the NBA. I'm impressed with the way he stands at attention for the National Anthem.

> — *Peter Vecsey, sportswriter*

He went from Cy Young to sayonara in one year.

> — *Graig Nettles, New York Yankees infielder, on the*
> *team's trade of Sparky Lyle to the Texas Rangers*

Out of what, a thousand?

> — *Mickey Rivers, New York Yankees outfielder, on being*
> *told teammate Reggie Jackson had an IQ of 140*

I'm in room 123. Go up and write a column and a sidebar.

> — *Woody Paige, sportswriter, to a woman in a bar who*
> *offered to do anything he wanted for $100*

Our kicker had one bad day last year. Saturday.

> — *Gary Darnell, Tennessee Tech football coach,*
> *after an 0-11 season*

Inflation killed the Vanderbilt Commodores Saturday. Once the football was inflated, Vanderbilt was dead.

> — *Jimmy Bryan, sportswriter*

I prefer fast food.

> — *Rocky Bridges, San Francisco Giants coach,*
> *on why he doesn't eat snails*

He's short, and we plan to make him shorter.

> — *Mike Ditka, Chicago Bears coach, on*
> *Los Angeles Rams quarterback Dieter Brock*

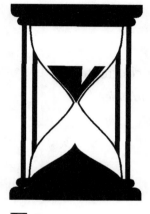

It takes him an hour and a half to watch *60 Minutes*.

> — *Donald Davidson, Houston Astros executive,*
> *on Joe Niekro, Astros pitcher*

I once scouted a pitcher who was so bad that when he came into the game, the ground crew dragged the warning track.

> — *Ellis Clary, Minnesota Twins scout*

First I found it hard to catch him. Then I found it hard to hit him. And finally I found it hard to manage him.

> — *Joe Torre, Atlanta Braves manager, on Phil Niekro*

It was an insurance run, so I hit it to the Prudential building.

> — *Reggie Jackson, New York Yankees outfielder,*
> *on a long home run at Fenway Park*

John Elway is a great football player. He used to be my son. Now I'm his father.

> — *Jack Elway, San Jose State University football coach*

The most difficult shot? I find it to be the hole-in-one.

> — *Groucho Marx, comedian*

METAPHORS & SIMILES

In baseball you hit a home run over the right field fence, the left field fence, the center field fence. Nobody cares. In golf, everything has got to be right over second base.

— Ken Harrelson, Cleveland Indians infielder

Mike Ivie is a forty-million dollar airport with a thirty-dollar control tower.

— Rick Monday, Los Angeles Dodgers outfielder

If Howard Cosell were a sport, he'd be roller derby.

— Jimmy Cannon, sportswriter

They must have been an expansion gang.

— Gene Mauch, Montreal Expos manager, on a battle between rival gangs that used faulty ammunition

We think of it as fuzzy concrete.

— John McKay, football coach at USC, commenting on artificial grass

Long relief is like being a plumber. Some days it's O.K., but when 30 septic tanks back up, it's no fun.

— George Frazier, Chicago Cubs relief pitcher

When you're hitting the ball, it comes at you looking like a grapefruit. When you're not, it looks like a black-eyed pea.

— George Scott, Boston Red Sox

Hitting at 5:15 P.M., with the shadows that are being cast, is like trying to swat flies with a string of spaghetti.

— Pete Rose, Cincinnati Reds infielder

He's like a little kid in a train station. You turn your back on him and he's gone.

> *— Doc Medich, Milwaukee Brewers pitcher,*
> *on Rickey Henderson, Oakland A's base stealer*

He plays the outfield like he's trying to catch grenades.

> *— Reggie Jackson, New York Yankees outfielder, on Atlanta*
> *Braves outfielder Claudell Washington*

Thinking you can win the Crosby Pro-Am with a high handicap makes as much sense as leaving the porch light on for Jimmy Hoffa.

> *— Phil Harris, entertainer*

Trying to hit him is like trying to eat Jell-O with chopsticks.

> *— Bobby Murcer, San Francisco Giants outfielder,*
> *on knuckleball pitcher Phil Niekro*

That's like Al Capone speaking out for gun control.

> *— Blackie Sherrod, sportswriter, on Ted Turner's*
> *complaint that player salaries were too high*

Hockey players are like mules: They have no fear of punishment and no hope of reward.

> *— Emory Jones, St. Louis Arena general manager*

You can't really tell anything. It's like seeing your daughter come in at 4 o'clock in the morning with a Gideon Bible.

> *— Don Farmbrough, Kansas football coach,*
> *on what you learn in spring practice*

I'm like a duck above water, but paddling like hell underneath.

> *— Frank Shero, Philadelphia Flyers coach*

I feel like a rat in a cheese factory with the cat on vacation.

> *— Thomas Henderson, Dallas Cowboys,*
> *on how it felt to win the Super Bowl*

UNDERSTATEMENTS

I've got one fault. I lie a lot.

> — *Tom Lasorda, Los Angeles Dodgers manager*

You have a turnover here and you've got trouble.

> — *Rick Sund, Dallas Mavericks official,*
> *watching a man juggling a chain saw*

I guess I was due for a bad outing.

> — *Bill Bonham, Chicago Cubs rookie pitcher, in his first*
> *outing. He failed to retire any of the batters*

I'm lucky if I own 200.

> — *Hank Stram, ex-NFL coach, about reports*
> *that he owns 400 suits*

MORE WORDS, WORDS, WORDS

Wally Joyner just completed an unassisted double play by himself.

> — *Ken Brett, California Angels announcer*

The Baltimore Orioles team is experiencing many problems this year collectively as a group.

> — *Ken Brett, California Angels announcer*

The average age of the Chicago White Sox team is 26 years per man.

> — *Ken Brett, California Angels announcer*

We have already had the plate umpire carried off the field barely under his own power.

> — *Ken Brett, California Angels announcer*

I said, "What can you tell me I don't know? I know the bases are loaded. I know we are leading by one run. I know I have 2 balls on the batter. I know I have to throw a strike. I know I have to try."

> — *Dan Stanhouse, Baltimore Orioles pitcher,*
> *when the coach came out to talk to him*

That'll be 50 bucks. Oh, I can't do that, can I?

> — *Butch Van Breda Kolff, ex NBA coach then coaching at*
> *Lafayette College, to a player who arrived late*

BOXING

Fighting is the only racket where you're almost guaranteed to end up a bum.

— *Rocky Graziano, former middleweight champion*

Boxing is a great sport and a dirty business.

— *Ken Norton, heavyweight boxer*

I have never been around so many crummy people in all my days.

— *Ed "Too Tall" Jones, Dallas Cowboys*
lineman, on his brief boxing career

If there's a wrinkle here and a straight deal there, the boxing crowd would go for the wrinkle every time.

— *Jerry Perenchio, boxing promoter*

You're damn right I know where I am. I'm in Madison Square Garden getting beaten up.

— *Willie Pastrano, light heavyweight fighter, after being*
knocked down, and asked if he knew where he was

I consider myself blessed. I consider you blessed. We're all blessed with God-given talents. Mine just happens to be beatin' up people.

— *Sugar Ray Leonard, talking to students at Harvard*

Lay down, so I can recognize you.

— *Willie Pep, on seeing some ex-fighters*

Instead of practicing boxing, he should have taken voice lessons, so he could have yelled for help.

— *Jackie Mason, comedian, advice to Michael Spinks*

In The Beginning

QUALIFICATIONS

The only qualifications for a lineman are to be big and dumb. To be a back you only have to be dumb.

> — *Knute Rockne, Notre Dame football coach*

My theory is that if you buy an ice cream cone and make it hit your mouth, you can play [tennis]. If you stick it on your forehead, your chances are less.

> — *Vic Braden, tennis instructor*

You have to be able to get up off the floor when you can't.

> — *Jack Dempsey, boxer*

Speed, strength, and the ability to recognize pain immediately.

> — *Reggie Williams, Cincinnati Bengals linebacker*

If you're too lazy to work and too chicken to steal, you become a bull rider.

> — *Charles Sampson, rodeo star*

First, you have to flunk an IQ test. Second, you have to be able to drink a gallon of beer. If you can drink more than a gallon, they give you a seat in the front row behind the Boston bullpen.

> — *Joe Sambito, Boston Red Sox relief pitcher,*
> *on how to qualify for seats in the bleachers*

It's a form of Oriental offensive grunting. If a man using karate has laryngitis, he is disarmed.

> — *Dr. Harold E. Kenney, Illinois*
> *wrestling coach, on karate*

There's nothing tough about playing third. All a guy needs is a strong arm and a strong chest.

> — *Frankie Frisch, Pittsburgh Pirates manager*

SCHOOLS AND GRADES

It was like a heart transplant. We tried to implant college in him, but his head rejected it.

> — *Barry Switzer, former Oklahoma football coach,*
> *on why a player had to quit college*

Son, looks to me like you're spending too much time on one subject.

> — *Shelby Metcalf, Texas A & M, advising a player*
> *whose grades were four F's and one D*

Monday through Friday they want you to be like Harvard. On Saturday, they want you to play like Oklahoma.

> — *Jim Valvano, North Carolina State basketball coach,*
> *on college administrators*

I never graduated from Iowa, but I was only there for two terms...Truman's and Eisenhower's.

> — *Alex Karras, Iowa football player*

It reflects the failure of our educational system.

> — *Steve Kreider, Cincinnati Bengals, when over*
> *46,000 fans came to a game, with the wind-chill*
> *factor of -50 degrees*

At N.C. State they had a big scandal. Three of the players were found in the library.

> — *Pat Williams, Philadelphia 76ers, on Jim Valvano,*
> *North Carolina State basketball coach*

Not all the juvenile delinquents are in the poolrooms. Some are in the classrooms.

> — *Jim McCaffey, Xavier University basketball coach*

Because the track coach was the biology teacher, and I had trouble with biology. I'm not crazy.

> — *Claudell Washington, NY Yankees,*
> *on why he was on the track team in high school*

There's one stipulation. The recipient must have a higher grade point average than I did.

> — *Jim Valvano, North Carolina State basketball coach, after he*
> *set up a $4,000 scholarship at his alma mater, Rutgers*

I don't know why people question the academic training of a student athlete. Half the doctors graduated in the bottom half of their class.

> — *Al McGuire, former basketball coach*

Auburn is giving Citrus Bowl tickets to tailback Brent Fullwood's profs so that they'll finally get to see him in person.

> — *Larry Guest, Orlando Sentinel writer*

He can move around pretty good. He just didn't move to class too well.

> — *Bill Yeoman, University of Houston, on 300 pound*
> *Earl Jones being ineligible because of poor grades*

I can't miss class. The prof doesn't have to call roll to know I'm not there.

> — *Tom Burleson, North Carolina State 7' center*

Well, we do have a draw play.

> — *Pat McInally, Cincinnati Bengals,*
> *on how art history helped in the NFL*

I asked the young man if he was in the top half of his class academically. He said, "No sir, I am one of those who make the top half possible."

> — *Pete Elliot, Miami University football coach,*
> *on a youngster he was recruiting*

RECRUITING

I try for good players and I try for good character. If necessary, though, I settle for the good player.

> — *Phil Maloney, Vancouver Canucks coach*

We have some good players in all sports, but if we have a losing season, I might have to go recruiting.

> — *Adolph Barela, New York State*
> *Penitentiary recreation supervisor*

Just give every coach the same amount of money and tell him he can keep what's left over.

> — *Abe Lemons, Oklahoma State basketball coach,*
> *on how to solve the recruiting problem*

When the athletic director said I should recruit more white players to keep the folks in Pullman happy, I signed Rufus White and Willie White.

> — *George Raveling, Washington State basketball coach*

Any kid who would leave that wonderful weather is too dumb to play for us.

> — *Alex Agase, Purdue football coach,*
> *why he doesn't try to get Californians*

I had one real good one in Florida to recruit. I really worked on the parents, believing it to be the way. Coach Bear Bryant of Alabama worked on the boy. I dined and danced with the boy's mother. The boy went to Alabama. The mother enrolled at Miami.

> — *Otis Mooney, Miami University football coach*

TRAINING & CONDITIONING

After the season with the Celtics, he said he couldn't pitch for the Red Sox for 4 weeks because it took him that long to get out of shape.

> — *Bill Russell, former Boston Celtic, on Gene Conley,*
> *who played for the Celtics and the Boston Red Sox*

Babe Ruth never stretched.

> — *Joaquin Andujar, Oakland A's pitcher,*
> *when he walked away from stretching exercises*

I spent 12 years training for a career that was over in a week. Joe Namath spent a week training for a career that lasted 12 years.

> — *Bruce Jenner, Olympic decathlon champion*

I flush the john between innings to keep my wrists strong.

> — *John Lowenstein, Baltimore Orioles reserve player,*
> *on how he keeps in shape*

TECHNIQUE
How to Play the Game

You hit home runs by not trying to hit home runs. I know that doesn't sound right, and it won't read right, but that's the way it is.

> — *Charlie Lau, hitting coach*

The way you catch a knuckleball is to wait until the ball stops rolling and then pick it up.

> — *Bob Uecker, sportscaster and former catcher*

There are two ways to catch a knuckleball. Unfortunately, neither of them works.

> — *Charlie Lau, batting coach*

Forecheck, backcheck, and paycheck.

> — *Gil Perreault, Buffalo Sabres,*
> *on three main parts of checking*

Look for the seams and then hit in-between them.

> — *Harmon Killebrew, Minnesota Twins,*
> *on hitting the knuckleball*

I grab a whole armful of guys with the other color jersey, and then I peel 'em off until I find the one with the ball.

> — *Big Daddy Lipscomb, Baltimore Colts lineman*

I throw the ball right down the middle. The high-ball hitters swing over it and the low ball hitters swing under it.

> — *Saul Rogovin, Chicago White Sox pitcher*

It's a round ball and a round bat, but you've got to hit it square.

— *Pete Rose, Cincinnati Reds infielder*

I zigged when I should have zagged.

— *Jack Roper, heavyweight contender,*
on being knocked out by Joe Louis

If a lot of people gripped a knife and fork like they do a golf club, they'd starve to death.

— *Sam Snead, professional golfer*

The hardest shot is a mashie at ninety yards from the green, where the ball has to be played against an oak tree, bounces back into a sandtrap, hits a stone, bounces on the green and then rolls into the cup. That shot is so difficult I have only made it once.

— *Zeppo Marx, comedian*

Hitting is timing. Pitching is upsetting timing.

— *Warren Spahn, Milwaukee Braves pitcher*

Pitching is the art of instilling fear by making a man flinch.

— *Sandy Koufax, Los Angeles Dodgers pitcher*

The art of hitting is the art of getting your pitch to hit.

— *Bobby Brown, New York Yankees infielder*

There's no such thing as an unimportant stolen base.

— *Maury Wills, Los Angeles Dodgers infielder*

HUMBLE BEGINNINGS

My family was so poor they couldn't afford kids. The lady next door had me.

> — *Lee Trevino, golf pro*

I got into a line one day in high school thinking it was a towel line. When they handed me a football suit, I was too shy to give it back.

> — *Eddie LeBaron, Dallas Cowboys star quarterback,*
> *on how his shyness got him into football*

I became a sportswriter because, back in my days at Time magazine, I was the only one in the building who could spell Yastrzemski.

> — *Jim Murray, Los Angeles Times columnist*

My friend Robert Delgado was a jockey. I saw that he drove a big Cadillac and had lots of girls.

> — *Rene Rieva, on why he became a jockey*

I hate homework.

> — *Mareen Louie, tennis player,*
> *on why she turned pro at 18*

ROOKIES/PROS

It was his best game yet, but he's still a rookie. He doesn't count. He's not even a person yet.

> — *Bill Russell, Sacramento Kings basketball coach,*
> *on rookie Kenny Smith*

Go out and knock down a veteran a few times. You're adults now.

> — *Norman Van Brocklin, Vikings football coach,*
> *on how rookies can make the team*

It's the difference between a carpenter and a cabinet-maker.

> — *Birdie Tebbetts, Cleveland Indians manager, on the*
> *differences between veteran pitchers and rookies*

The scouts said I looked like Tarzan and played like Jane.

> — *Dennis Harrison, 6'8" and 275 pounds rookie,*
> *drafted late by the Philadelphia Eagles*

My only goal right now is to win. That, and maybe start to shave.

> — *Johnny Moore, 17-year old Texas basketball player*

I saw the kid play at Wisconsin Rapids last year. I knew immediately he was doomed to become an all-star centerfielder.

> — *Calvin Griffith, Minnesota Twins owner,*
> *on Jim Eisenreich*

ADVICE TO ROOKIES & PLAYERS

Don't bother reading it kid. Everybody gets killed in the end.

> — *Peter Gent, former Dallas Cowboy,*
> *describing coach Tom Landry's playbook to a rookie*

Throw high risers at the chin; throw peas at the knees; throw it here when they're lookin' there; throw it there when they're lookin' here.

> — *Satchel Paige, Negro Leagues pitcher*

When you're on a sleeper at night, take your pocketbook and put it in a sock under your pillow. That way, the next morning you won't forget your pocketbook 'cause you'll be looking for your sock.

> — *Ping Bodie, New York Yankees outfielder*

The best way to pitch to Stan Musial? That's easy: walk him and then try to pick him off first base.

> — *Joe Garagiola, Pittsburgh Pirates catcher*

Get in front of those balls — you won't get hurt. That's what you've got a chest for, young man.

> — *John McGraw, New York Giants manager*

Run everything out and be in by twelve.

> — *Red Schoendienst, St. Louis Cardinals manager*

Never trust a baserunner who's limping. Comes a base hit and you'll think he just got back from Lourdes.

> — *Joe Garagiola, sportscaster*

Don't forget to swing hard, in case you hit the ball.

> — *Woodie Held, Cleveland Indians infielder*

Never win 20 games, because then they'll expect you to do it every year.
> — *Billy Loes, Brooklyn Dodgers pitcher*

Win any way you can as long as you can get away with it.
> — *Leo Durocher, Brooklyn Dodgers manager*

Be quick, but never hurry.
> — *John Wooden, UCLA basketball coach*

Relax your muscles when you can. Relaxing your brain is fatal.
> — *Stirling Moss, race driver*

Take the shortest possible route to the ball carrier, and arrive in a bad humor.
> — *Bowden Wyatt, University of Tennessee football coach*

If you ever get belted and see three different fighters through a haze, go after the one in the middle.
> — *Max Baer, former heavyweight champion*

When I first became a manager, I asked Chuck [Tanner] for advice. He told me, "Always rent."
> — *Tony La Russa, Chicago White Sox manager*

Don't ever ask a player to do something he doesn't have the ability to do, because he'll question your ability as a coach, not his as an athlete.
> — *Lou Holtz, University of Arkansas football coach*

If you want to whip somebody on the golf course, just get him mad.
> — *Dave Williams, University of Houston golf coach*

Never bet with anyone you meet on the first tee who has a deep suntan, a one-iron in his bag and squinty eyes.
> — *Dave Marr, professional golfer*

Do not allow yourself to be annoyed because your opponent insists on making elaborate study of all his putts.

> — *Horace G. Hutchinson,* Hints on the Game of Golf

If you are going to throw a club, it is important to throw it ahead of you, down the fairway, so you don't waste energy going back to pick it up.

> — *Tommy Bolt, professional golfer*

Look like a woman, but play like a man.

> — *Jan Stephenson, professional golfer*

Make the hard ones look easy and the easy ones look hard.

> — *Walter Hagen, professional golfer*

When you're a professional, you come back, no matter what happened the day before.

> — *Billy Martin, New York Yankees manager*

Avoid fried foods which angry up the blood. If your stomach disputes you, lie down and pacify it with cool thoughts. Keep the juices flowing by jangling around gently as you move. Go very light on the vices such as carrying on in society — the social ramble ain't restful. Avoid running at all times. Don't look back — something might be gaining on you.

> — *Satchel Paige*

A runner must understand that there's one bad thing about carrying that football—it attracts a crowd.

> — *John McKay, University of Southern California football coach*

Just take the ball and throw it where you want to. Throw strikes. Home plate don't move.

> — *Satchel Paige, pitcher, explaining how to pitch*

Ask Me No Questions

Mike Ditka doesn't tell Tom Landry how to beat the Bears.

— *Martina Navratilova, tennis pro, answering*
if she gave advice to opposing players

Under an assumed name.

> — *Dutch Harrison, golf pro, when a golfer*
> *asked how he should play the next ball*

The first thing is to become 7' tall.

> — *Wilt Chamberlain, 7'1" basketball center,*
> *on how to become a basketball star*

Grow an inch.

> — *Spud Webb, 5'7" basketball player on the*
> *Atlanta Hawks, to a 5'6" reporter, on how he*
> *could learn to dunk*

Take your bat with you.

> — *Earl Weaver, advice to Al Bumbry,*
> *who was in a slump and going to church*

Business is Business

Outrageous FORTUNES
Dollars & Cents

Man, if I made a million dollars I would come in at six in the morning, sweep the stands, wash the uniforms, clean out the offices, manage the team and play the game.

> — *Duke Snider, former Brooklyn Dodgers outfielder*

No player is worth a million dollars. I can understand why a player would have an agent. I couldn't keep from laughing if I went in and demanded a million dollars from an owner.

> — *Red Grange, former Chicago Bears running back*

I'm going to write a book, **How to Make a Small Fortune in Baseball**. First, you start with a large fortune.

> — *Robert Carpenter III, Philadelphia Phillies owner*

 **A**ll last year we tried to teach him English and the only word he learned was "million."

> — *Tommy Lasorda, L.A. Dodgers manager,*
> *on Fernando Valenzuela's salary expectations*

I don't think Johnny Carson got a lot of hate mail when he signed for $5 million. But Bruce Sutter probably did. Why? Well, Johnny is a lot funnier than Bruce. I mean, Bruce is a wonderful guy, but his Karnak is weak.

> — *Steve Stone, Baltimore Orioles pitcher*

What the hell's the matter with a society that offers a football coach a million dollars?

> — *Joe Paterno, on turning down a million dollars*
> *to coach the New England Patriots*

THE COLOR OF MONEY

Anyone who says they're not in it for the money is full of shit.

— *Fred Biletnikoff, Oakland Raiders receiver*

The great trouble with baseball today is that most of the players are in the game for the money that's in it—not for the love of it, the excitement of it, the thrill of it.

— *Ty Cobb*

Baseball has prostituted itself. Pretty soon we'll be starting games at midnight so the people in outer space can watch on prime-time television. We're making a mistake by always going for more money.

— *Ray Kroc, San Diego Padres owner*

Branch Rickey had both money and players. He just didn't like to see the two of them to mix.

— *Chuck Connors, former Brooklyn Dodgers infielder*

I got a million dollars' worth of advice and a small raise.

— *Ed Stanky, former Dodger,*
after meeting with Branch Rickey

Eric Dickerson has found a miracle cure for thigh bruises, just rub it with money.

— *Charlie Jones, NBC commentator*

Beer makes some people happy. Winning ball games makes some people happy. Cashing checks makes me delirious with joy.

— *Jim Brosnan, Cincinnati Reds pitcher*

I'm the most loyal player money can buy.

> — *Don Sutton, California Angels pitcher*

Ninety percent I'll spend on good times, women and whiskey. The other 10 percent I'll probably waste.

> — *Tug McGraw, Philadelphia Phillies pitcher*

He throws nickels around like they were manhole covers.

> — *Mike Ditka, Chicago Bears tight end,*
> *on team owner George Halas.*

They say money talks, but the only thing it ever says to me is goodbye.

> — *Paul Waner, Pittsburgh Pirates outfielder*

The Cadillacs are down at the end of the bat.

> — *Ralph Kiner, former Pittsburgh Pirates outfielder,*
> *on why he didn't choke up*

We're still about two Cadillacs apart.

> — *Ken Holtzman, Chicago Cubs pitcher,*
> *on his salary dispute*

Taters, that's where the money is.

> — *Reggie Jackson, New York Yankees outfielder*

A homer a day will boost my pay.

> — *Josh Gibson, Negro League catcher*

The actuarial tables show that linemen in this game die at the age of 53. I start collecting my pension at 55. Nice.

> — *Bill Bain, Los Angeles Rams lineman*

Live in it, wear it, and eat it.

> — *Ticky Burden, Utah Stars draft choice,*
> *on how he would spend his bonus*

I really don't like talking about money. All I can say is that the Good Lord must have wanted me to have it.

> — *Larry Bird, Boston Celtics forward*

With the money I'm making, I should be playing two positions.

> — *Pete Rose, Philadelphia Phillies infielder*

Pete doesn't count his money anymore, he weighs it.

> — *Stan Musial, former St. Louis Cardinals infielder*

You writers seem fascinated to see black fighters go broke. You write that it's terrible that poor Joe Louis is broke. Well, Rolls Royce is broke. The Penn Central is broke. The Catholic schools is broke.

> — *Muhammad Ali*

There are no rich Mexicans. They get some money, they call themselves Spanish.

> — *Lee Trevino, professional golfer*

I can't say just what I'll ask for, but it's going to take a $600,000 man to stop O.J. Simpson.

> — *Joe Green, on being drafted in the NFL*

I look at the ball, and I see dollar signs instead of stitches.

> — *Carl Furillo, Brooklyn Dodgers outfielder*

Sam Snead's got more money buried underground than I ever made on top. He's got gophers in his backyard that subscribe to *Fortune*. He's packed more coffee cans than Brazil.

> — *Arnold Palmer, professional golfer*

Too much money involved. When not so much money, not any problems.

> — *Ilie Nastase, professional tennis player,*
> *on the chaotic state of professional tennis*

The dollars aren't so important. Once you have them.

> — *Johnny Miller, professional golfer*

A ballplayer's got to be kept hungry to become a big leaguer. That's why no boy from a rich family ever made the big leagues.

> — *Joe Di Maggio, New York Yankees outfielder*

With the salary I get here, I'm so hollow and starving that I'm liable to explode like a light bulb if I hit the ground too hard.

> — *Casey Stengel, Pittsburgh Pirates outfielder*

I was only in the majors two months before I got a raise. The minimum went up.

> — *Bob Uecker,* Catcher in the Wry

It's tough to sit in that on-deck circle making $800,000 less than the guy hitting in front of you.

> — *Reggie Jackson, New York Yankees outfielder,*
> *on teammate Dave Winfield*

I'm getting $300,000, but over a 150-year period.

> — *Denny Crum, University of Louisville basketball coach*

He had a Puritan distaste for money in someone else's hands.

> — *Roger Kahn, sportswriter,*
> *on Branch Rickey, Brooklyn Dodgers executive*

I made $7,000 on the tour and spent $100,000. The IRS man sent me a get-well card.

> — *Chi Chi Rodriguez, professional golfer*

I don't mind paying a player, but I don't want to pay for his funeral.

> — *Pat Gillick, Toronto Blue Jays executive, on a*
> *40-year-old player's demand for a multi-year contract*

When we played, World Series checks meant something. Now all they do is screw up your taxes.

> — *Don Drysdale, former Los Angeles Dodgers pitcher*

I was a bonus baby. I got two autographed baseballs and a scorecard from the 1935 All-Star Game.

> — *Bob Feller, Cleveland Indians pitcher*

Today's salaries are way out of line. If they continue to escalate like they are, the only people who will be able to afford to buy tickets will be the players and their agents.

> — *Zollie Volchok, Seattle Super*
> *Sonics general manager*

It's changed so much. They sign for bonuses: If you know where home plate is, $50,000. If you know where first base is, $25,000.

> — *Joe Garagiola, sportscaster*

I believe there are certain things that cannot be bought: loyalty, friendship, health, love and an American League pennant.

> — *Edward Bennett Williams, Baltimore Orioles owner*

We will scheme, connive, steal and do everything possible to win a pennant. Everything except pay big salaries.

> — *Bill Veeck, Chicago White Sox owner*

I measure it by Cadillacs. I used to pay $5,000 for mine. They pay $20,000 now. So, if they make three times as much as I did, what's the difference?

> — *Mickey Mantle, former New York Yankees outfielder*

When I got out of the army I signed with Milwaukee for a three thousand dollar bonus. The amount bothered my father at first. We were a poor family and, frankly, he didn't have that kind of cash.

— *Bob Uecker,* Catcher in the Wry

My father looked at the money, then glanced at my seven brothers and sisters. He couldn't contain himself. He said, "For five hundred dollars you can take the whole family."

— *Joe Dugan, Philadelphia Athletics infielder,
on signing for a bonus*

When I played in Brooklyn, I could go to the ballpark for a nickel carfare. But now I live in Pasadena, and it costs me $15 to take a cab to Glendale. If I was a young man, I'd study to become a cab driver.

— *Casey Stengel, former New York Yankees manager*

I don't mind the high price of stardom, I just don't like the high price of mediocrity.

— *Bill Veeck, Chicago White Sox owner*

You can never overpay a good player. You can only overpay a bad one. I don't mind paying a good player $200,000. What I mind is paying a $20,000 player $22,000.

— *Art Rooney, Pittsburgh Steelers owner*

One year I hit .291 and had to take a salary cut. If you hit .291 today, you'd own the franchise.

— *Enos Slaughter, former St. Louis Cardinals outfielder*

Isn't it amazing that we're worth so much on the trading block and worth so little when we talk salary with the general manager?

— *Jim Kern, Texas Rangers pitcher*

I didn't think I could give the Yankees a $100,000 year.

— *Joe Di Maggio, on why he retired*

It's a lot tougher to get up in the mornings when you start wearing silk pajamas.

> — *Eddie Arcaro, former jockey*

The problem is, I'm already two million in spending.

> — *Chi Chi Rodriguez, golf pro,*
> *nearing a million dollars in earnings*

Every time I look at my pocketbook, I see Jackie Robinson.

> — *Willie Mays, New York Giants outfielder*

There are two things I've never wanted to be, real rich or real poor. Being a football coach enables me to do it.

> — *Lou Holtz, University of Notre Dame football coach*

I really love that kid.

> — *Calvin Griffith, Minnesota Twins owner, after*
> *his catcher Butch Wynegar said he loved the game*
> *so much he'd play for nothing*

I do not like football well enough to play it for nothing.

> — *Red Grange, former Chicago Bears running back*

If I wanted to meet millionaires, I don't have to go anywhere. I just look up my own players.

> — *Walter O'Malley, L.A. Dodger owner,*
> *invited to meet some millionaires*

Guys who play there say it gets awfully lonely. Hell, for the money they're talking, I can buy some friends and take them with me.

> — *Reggie Jackson, on being offered*
> *more than one million dollars to play in Japan*

I'm not going to quit a $70,000 job to go to work.

> — *Norm Cash, Detroit Tigers first baseman,*
> *on when he would quit*

That means I work without pay.

> — *Moose Krause, former Notre Dame athletic directer,*
> *on his title of athletic director emeritus*

I like the thought of playing for money instead of silverware. I never did like to polish.

> — *Patty Sheehan, new to the LPGA*

Every time I see my mother I say, "Why didn't you wait?"

> — *Rod Hundley, who had signed for $10,000 salary*
> *when he was drafted by the NBA*

Not really, they lean toward cash.

> — *Bill Veeck, Chicago White Sox owner,*
> *if free agents preferred Chicago to other cities*

I read where he was embarrassed by the $4.5 million Atlanta offer. I didn't want to add to his embarrassment.

> — *Tom Grieve, Texas Rangers general manager,*
> *on why he didn't try to sign Bob Horner*

Yeah. At the bank.

> — *Jim Rice, Boston Red Sox, with many injuries,*
> *if there was a place where he wasn't hurting*

If you expect a miracle, you should expect to pay for one.

> — *Derek Hardy, golf pro, who charges $1,000 for one lesson and only $140 for 13 lessons*

If you don't make the All-Star team, why am I paying you all this money?

> — *Stan Kasten, Atlanta Hawks GM, when highly-paid Dominque Wilkins asked for a bonus, if he made the All-Star team*

I'm so poor I can't even pay attention.

> — *Ron Kittle, NY Yankees DH, on his pay*

When Sam Mele, my nephew, is playing the Yanks or the Orioles I root for him. But when it comes down to the big thing, you know how I'm rooting. Money is thicker than blood.

> — *Tony Cuccinello, Chicago White Sox coach, when Sam Mele was manager of the Minnesota Twins*

I am, unless I got short-changed during the past 24 hours.

> — *Eddie Arcaro, jockey, responding to the inquiry if he were a millionaire*

He's the best rebounder in the Washington area, ain't he?

> — *Charles Barkley, Philadelphia 76ers basketball player, when asked about Moses Malone being the highest paid person in Washington D.C.*

When we couldn't get our uniforms out of the cleaners.

> — *Lou Rymkus, Akron Vulcans coach, at what point he realized his team had financial problems*

If people say I'm broke that's OK. Then maybe some of my friends will stop asking me for money.

> — *Roberto Duran, boxer, on rumors that he is broke*

AGENTS & CONTRACTS

I think an agent should get paid by the hour. I don't believe anyone should own a percentage of anyone else. That's one of the reasons we fought the Civil War.

> *— Al McGuire, Marquette*
> *basketball coach*

A complete ballplayer today is one who can hit, field, run, throw and pick the right agent.

> *— Bob Lurie, San Francisco Giants owner*

I don't need an agent. Why should I give someone ten percent when I do all the work?

> *— Mark "The Bird" Fidrych, Detroit Tigers pitcher*

I have a lifetime contract now. Of course, as soon as you start losing, you lose your life. They declare you legally dead.

> *— Dan Reeves, Denver Broncos football coach*

He signed me to a multi-day contract.

> *— Pat Williams, Philadelphia 76ers executive,*
> *on his relationship with owner Harold Katz*

I wouldn't do this for my health.

> *— Larry Holmes, on why he signed to fight Mike Tyson*

They made me an offer I could afford to refuse.

> *— Rod Laver, tennis pro, on his contract*
> *with the Los Angeles Strings*

THE FANS — THE FANATICS

I have discovered, in twenty years of moving around a ball park, that the knowledge of the game is usually in inverse proportion to the price of the seats.

— *Bill Veeck, Chicago White Sox owner*

Every player, in his secret heart, wants to manage someday. Every fan, in the privacy of his mind, already does.

— *Leonard Koppett, A Thinking Man's Guide to Baseball*

There are three things the average man thinks he can do better than anybody else: build a fire, run a hotel and manage a baseball team.

— *Rocky Bridges, Cincinnati Reds infielder*

My definition of a fan is the kind of guy who will scream at you from the 60th row of the bleachers because he thinks you missed a marginal holding call in the center of the interior line, and then after the game won't be able to find his car in the parking lot.

— *Jim Tunney, NFL referee*

Why, certainly, I'd like to have a fellow who hits a home run every time at bat, who strikes out every opposing batter when he's pitching, and who is always thinking about two innings ahead. The only trouble is to get him to put down his cup of beer, come down out of the stands and do those things.

— *Danny Murtaugh, Pittsburgh Pirates manager*

The majority of American males put themselves to sleep by striking out the batting order of the New York Yankees.

— *James Thurber, writer*

At Yankee Stadium the fans throw bottles from the outfield. At Comiskey Park, they throw them from the box seats.

— *Eddie Einhorn, Chicago White Sox owner*

Rooting for the Yankees is like rooting for U.S. Steel.

— *Joe E. Lewis, comedian*

Hating the Yankees is as American as pizza pie, unwed mothers and cheating on your income tax.

— *Mike Royko, writer*

I never have been on a yacht in my whole life. But I imagine rooting for the Yankees is like owning a yacht.

— *Jimmy Cannon, sportswriter*

You can talk all you like about Brooklyn and New York, Minneapolis and St. Paul, Dallas and Fort Worth, but there are no two cities in America where the people want to beat each other's brains out more than in San Francisco and Los Angeles.

— *Joe Cronin, Boston Red Sox manager*

Being a White Sox fan meant measuring victory in terms of defeat. A 6-5 defeat was a good day. A big rally was Wally Moses doubling down the right field line.

— *Jean Shepherd, writer*

I love signing autographs. I'll sign anything but veal cutlets. My ball point pen slips on veal cutlets.

— *Casey Stengel, New York Yankees manager*

The Good Lord wants the Cubs to win!

— *Harry Caray, Chicago Cubs announcer,*
on a game-winning double play

One thing you learn as a Cubs fan: When you bought your ticket, you could bank on seeing the bottom of the ninth.

— *Joe Garagiola, sportscaster*

Philadelphia fans would boo funerals, an Easter egg hunt, a parade of armless war vets and the Liberty Bell.

> — *Bo Belinsky, Philadelphia Phillies pitcher*

If the fans don't want to come out to the park, nobody can stop 'em.

> — *Yogi Berra, New York Yankees catcher*

Fans don't boo nobodies.

> — *Reggie Jackson, New York Yankees outfielder*

When I'm on the road, my greatest ambition is to get a standing boo.

> — *Al Hrabosky, St. Louis Cardinals relief pitcher*

I played the game the same every time because I was playing for the fans, not for me. It's their game.

> — *Willie Mays, former San Francisco Giants outfielder*

There's a different breed of cats coming out here. Instead of hoi polloi, we're now getting Johnny Six-Pack.

> — *Mike Blanchard, Forest Hills referee,*
> *on modern tennis fans*

You can tell interest has increased in the Southwest basketball conference this season. They've already hung two coaches in effigy.

> — *Glenn Rose, Arkansas basketball coach*

Smoking shortens your life by eight years. I love to watch pro football on TV. If I smoke I'll miss 300 games.

> — *Tony Curtis, actor and football fan,*
> *on why he gave up smoking*

I know we're playing 11 games, our players know we're playing 11 games, but our fans think we're playing one game...Notre Dame.

> — *Charles McClendon, LSU football coach*

FOOTBALL

If you really like the game and go about it with unabashed enthusiasm, then you play better. By unabashed enthusiasm, I mean going crazy.

> — *John Matuszak, Houston Oilers football player*

Pro football is a mean game, ideally played by mean men. If it builds character, so does street mugging.

> — *Larry King, TV host*

Pro football gave me a good sense of perspective to enter politics. I'd already been booed, cheered, cut, sold, traded and hung in effigy.

> — *Jack Kemp, Congressman and former Buffalo Bills quarterback*

It's committee meetings, called huddles, separated by outbursts of violence.

> — *George Will, political commentator*

Football doesn't build character, it eliminates the weak ones.

> — *Darrell Royal, University of Texas football coach*

This isn't nuclear physics, it's a game. How smart do you really have to be?

> — *Terry Bradshaw, Pittsburgh Steelers quarterback*

Some people try to find things in this game that don't exist. Football is two things: blocking and tackling.

> — *Vince Lombardi, Green Bay Packers coach*

I never tried to keep football simple. If your offense is simple, it's simple to stop. If your defense is simple, it's simple to attack. Simple things are for simple people.

> — *John Madden,* Hey, Wait a Minute (I Wrote a Book!)

The Powers That Be

COACHES & MANAGERS
On Again-Gone Again

Managing is like holding a dove in your hand. Squeeze too hard and you kill it; not hard enough and it flies away.

— *Tom Lasorda, Los Angeles Dodgers manager*

Coaches are like politicians: they have to be smart enough to understand the game, but dumb enough to think it's important.

— *Eugene McCarthy, former United States Senator*

There are two kinds of coaches: them that's just been fired and them that's going to be fired.

— *Bum Phillips, Houston Oilers coach*

If you don't win, you're going to be fired. If you do win, you've only put off the day you're going to be fired.

— *Leo Durocher,* Nice Guys Finish Last

Winning is the name of the game. The more you win, the less you get fired.

— *Bep Guidolin, Boston Bruins coach*

Managing a ball club is a job for which a man works, studies, hopes and, if he's gaited that way, prays—knowing all the time that if he gets it, he's bound, in the end, to be fired.

— *Birdie Tebbetts, Cleveland Indians manager*

If you want job security, drive a mail truck.

— *Alvin Dark, former San Francisco Giants manager*

When a coach is hired, he's fired. The date just hasn't been filled in yet.

— *C.W. Newton, Alabama basketball coach*

Do you know what the average tenure is among big league managers? Two and a half years. Migrant fruit picking is more secure than that.

— *Bob Uecker,* Catcher in the Wry

They give you a new Cadillac one year, and the next year they give you the gas to get out of town.

— *Woody Hayes, Ohio State football coach*

Behind every fired football coach stands a college president.

— *John McKay, University of Southern
California football coach*

No athletic director holds office longer than two unsuccessful football coaches.

— *Bob Zupke, University of Illinois football coach*

Few die on the job.

— *Wellington Mara, New York Giants owner*

The first thing we look for in a house is its resale value.

— *Mrs. Lou Holtz*

A lifetime contract for a coach means if you're ahead in the third quarter and moving the ball, they can't fire you.

— *Lou Holtz, University of Arkansas football coach*

If you want to drop off the face of the earth, just be an assistant coach.

— *Bob Griese, former Miami Dolphins quarterback*

I can honestly say I will be the first president of a corporation to come into power upon the death, resignation or impeachment of the vice-president.

— *Edward Bennett Williams, Washington Redskins
owner and president, on vice-president and coach,
Vince Lombardi*

I had a friend with a lifetime contract. After two bad years, the university president called him into his office and pronounced him dead.

— *Bob Devaney, University of Nebraska football coach*

I can think of three managers who weren't fired. John McGraw of the Giants, who was sick and resigned; Miller Huggins of the Yankees, who died on the job; and Connie Mack of the Athletics, who owned the club.

— *Red Smith, sportswriter*

The only real way to know you've been fired is when you arrive at the ballpark and find your name has been scratched off the parking list.

— *Billy Martin, New York Yankees manager*

I've never thought of leaving Arkansas since I got here. Suicide yes, leaving no.

— *Lou Holtz, University of Arkansas football coach*

When I got into the coaching business, I knew I was getting into a high-risk, high-profile profession, so I adopted a philosophy I've never wavered from: Yesterday is a canceled check, today is cash on the line, tomorrow is a promissory note.

— *Hank Stram, former Kansas City Chiefs coach*

Between owners and players, a manager today has become a wishbone.

— *John Curtis, San Francisco Giants pitcher*

The problem here is to win just enough to keep the alumni sullen instead of mutinous.

— *Herman Hickman, Yale football coach*

Cattle have no alumni.

— *Phil Chutchin, former Oklahoma State University football coach, on why he quit coaching to raise cattle*

To be a good coach, you have to be the opposite of what you feel. When your team is going bad, you want to get on their ass but that's when everybody else is on their ass. Their family, their friends, the fans, the media, the guy in the grocery store. That's when you need to pat 'em on the back, to tell 'em to just keep working hard and everything will be all right. Conversely, when everything is going good, you don't have to pat 'em on the back because everybody else is. That's when you have to be tough.

> — *Vince Lombardi, Green Bay Packers coach,*
> *quoted by John Madden in* Hey, Wait a Minute
> (I Wrote a book!)

Coaching is kind of like smoking—it's not good for us.

> — *Jim Gudger, East Texas State*
> *University basketball coach*

All coaches religiously carry fungo bats in the spring to ward off suggestions that they are not working.

> — *Jim Brosnan, major league pitcher*

A coach isn't as smart as they say he is when he wins, or as stupid when he loses.

> — *Darrell Royal, University of Texas football coach*

Don't raise your boy to be a football coach. In fact, be more cautious than that. At the first sign of his desire to become a football coach, just stop raising him.

> — *Emmett Watson, writer*

The best way to test a Timex watch would be to tie it to Earl Weaver's tongue.

> — *Marty Springstead, major league umpire*

Coaches are an integral part of every manager's team, especially if they're good pinochle players.

> — *Earl Weaver, Baltimore Orioles manager*

We've got the worst in this league: Earl Weaver, Billy Martin, Ralph Houk, Gene Mauch—you name them, they're all maniacs. You can't reason with those guys. You don't try.

> — *Jim McKean, American League umpire*

Playing for Yogi [Berra] is like playing for your father; playing for Billy [Martin] is like playing for your father-in-law.

> — *Don Baylor, New York Yankees designated hitter*

Coaches think everybody is talking about them. They don't realize they're just a coffee break. The only time people at Equitable Life or Sperry Rand talk about them is when they're eating Danish. They all have their own problems.

> — *Al McGuire, Marquette basketball coach*

There are three things everybody in America thinks they can do better than anyone else: make love, be President, and coach a football team.

> — *George Young, New York Giants general manager*

No coach ever won a game by what he knows; it's what his players have learned.

> — *Amos Alonzo Stagg, college football coach*

If a coach starts listening to the fans, he winds up sitting next to them.

> — *Johnny Kerr, NBA coach*

When you're a coach, you're miserable. When you're not a coach, you're more miserable.

> — *Fred Shero, Philadelphia Flyers coach*

A manager really gets paid for how much he suffers.

> — *Gabe Paul, Cleveland Indians president*

I always tell the quarterback never to look at me for a play in a third and long situation. After all, he's on a four-year scholarship and I'm sittin' here with a one-year contract.

— *Frank Broyles, football coach*

They say all the breaks even up in the long run, but how many of us last that long?

— *Chuck Knox, Buffalo Bills coach*

I don't like all those TV time-outs. I run out of things to say to my team.

— *Jim Valvano, North Carolina State University basketball coach*

Twenty-five or thirty years ago a player came to you as a player. Now he comes to you as a corporation.

— *Bill Russell, basketball coach*

Open up a ballplayer's head and you know what you'd find? A lot of little broads and a jazz band.

— *Mayo Smith, Philadelphia Phillies manager*

Tell a ballplayer something a thousand times, then tell him again, because that might be the time he'll understand something.

— *Paul Richards, Baltimore Orioles manager*

You could tell five guys to go over to the post office at two o'clock and one of 'em wouldn't be there, so why have so many tricky plays?

— *Abe Lemons, University of Texas basketball coach*

I had no trouble communicating. The players just didn't like what I had to say.

— *Frank Robinson, former Cleveland Indians manager*

Coaches who can outline plays on a blackboard are a dime a dozen. The ones who win get inside their players and motivate.

— *Vince Lombardi, Green Bay Packers coach*

The main thing is getting people to play. When you think it's your system that's winning, you're in for a damn big surprise. It's those players' efforts.

— Bum Phillips, Houston Oilers coach

As soon as a coach begs, "Please, please play for me," he becomes a whore. Don't play hard for me. Play hard for yourself. If you don't want to, fine, but if we lose, don't come sobbing to me.

— John McKay, University of Southern
California football coach

I like my players to be married and in debt. That's the way you motivate them.

— Ernie Banks, Chicago Cubs coach

I want my teams to have my personality—surly, obnoxious and arrogant.

— Al McGuire, Marquette University basketball coach

A head coach is guided by this main objective: dig, claw, wheedle, coax that fanatical effort out of the players. You want them to play every Saturday as if they were planting the flag on Iwo Jima.

— Darrell Royal, University of Texas football coach

There are two ways to build a team. You either get better players or get the players you've got to play better.

— Bum Phillips, Houston Oilers coach

There will be two buses leaving the hotel for tomorrow night's game. The two P.M. bus will be for those of you who need a little extra work. The empty bus will leave at five P.M.

— Dave Bristol, San Francisco Giants manager,
to his players after a loss

I'm not the manager because I'm always right, but I'm always right because I'm the manager.

— Gene Mauch, California Angels manager

Whenever I decided to release a guy, I always had his room searched first for a gun. You couldn't take any chances with some of them birds.

> — *Casey Stengel, Brooklyn Dodger manager*

Most coaches study the films when they lose. I study them when we win, to see if I can figure out what I did right.

> — *Bear Bryant, Alabama football coach*

Football doesn't take me away from my family life. We've always watched films together.

> — *Fred Akers, University of Texas football coach*

There are coaches who spend 18 hours a day coaching the perfect game, and they lose because the ball is oval and they can't control the bounce.

> — *Bud Grant, Minnesota Vikings coach*

Nobody should work all the time. Everyone should have some leisure. I believe the early morning hours are best for this—the five or six hours when you're asleep.

> — *George Allen, Washington Redskins coach*

Coaches who shoot par in the summer are the guys I want on my schedule in the winter.

> — *Abe Lemons, University of Texas basketball coach*

The worst thing about managing is the day you realize you want to win more than the players do.

> — *Gene Mauch, California Angels manager*

The toughest thing about managing is standing up for nine innings.

> — *Paul Owens, Philadelphia Phillies manager*

If you make every game a life-and-death proposition, you're going to have problems. For one thing, you'll be dead a lot.

> — *Dean Smith, University of North Carolina basketball coach*

I'm going to become a hog farmer. After some of the things I've been through, I regard it as a step up.

— *Al Conover, Rice football coach*

I'd rather be a football coach. That way you can lose only 11 games a season. I lost 11 games in December alone.

— *Abe Lemons, Pan American College basketball coach*

Most managers are lifetime .220 hitters. For years, pitchers have been getting those managers out seventy-five percent of the time, and that's why they don't like us.

— *Bill Lee, Montreal Expos pitcher*

All managers are losers; they're the most expendable pieces of furniture on earth.

— *Ted Williams, Washington Senators manager*

When we lose I can't sleep at night. When we win I can't sleep at night, but when you win, you wake up feeling better.

— *Joe Torre, New York Mets manager*

A manager's job is simple. For 162 games, you try not to screw up all that smart stuff your organization did last December.

— *Earl Weaver, Baltimore Orioles manager*

A manager probably makes more decisions in the course of one game than a businessman makes in an entire week.

— *Tom Lasorda, Los Angeles Dodgers manager*

Out of twenty-five guys there should be five who would run through a wall for you, two or three who don't like you at all, five who are indifferent and maybe three undecided. My job is to keep the last two groups from going the wrong way.

— *Billy Martin, New York Yankees manager*

The secret of managing is to keep the guys who hate you away from the guys who are undecided.

> — *Casey Stengel*

They say I have to get to know my players. That arithmetic is bad. Isn't it simpler for twenty-five of them to get to know me?

> — *Birdie Tebbetts, Cleveland Indians manager*

I left because of illness and fatigue: the fans were sick and tired of me.

> — *John Ralston, former Denver Broncos coach,*
> *on why he left the team*

I don't mind starting a season with unknowns. I just don't like finishing a season with a bunch of 'em.

> — *Lou Holtz, University of Arkansas football coach*

A good coach needs a patient wife, a loyal dog and a great quarterback—not necessarily in that order.

> — *Bud Grant, Minnesota Vikings coach*

Lombardi treats us all the same—like dogs.

> — *Henry Jordan, Green Bay Packers lineman,*
> *on coach Vince Lombardi*

There is Eastern Standard Time and Greenwich Time, and then there is Lombardi Time—fifteen minutes early. If you come ten minutes early, they've started without you.

> — *Don Chandler, Green Bay Packers kicker*

One night, after a long, cold, difficult day, Lombardi came home late and tumbled into bed. "God," his wife said, "your feet are cold.'" And Lombardi answered, "Around the house, dear, you may call me Vince."

> — *Paul Hornung, Green Bay Packers running back*

He drives you until you know you can't go on. My legs just wouldn't come up anymore. When he walked by me, he hit them. He pushes you to the end of your endurance and then beyond it. If you have a reserve, he finds it.

— Henry Jordan, Green Bay Packers lineman,
on coach Vince Lombardi

When he says sit down, I don't even bother to look for a chair.

— Max McGee, Green Bay Packers receiver,
on Coach Lombardi

He's a perfectionist. If he was married to Raquel Welch, he'd expect her to cook.

— Don Meredith, sportscaster and former
Dallas Cowboys quarterback, on coach Tom Landry

Most coaches kick you in the butt one minute and pat you on the back the next. Rupp just kicked you in the butt all the time.

— Dan Issel, former player, on Adolph Rupp,
former University of Kentucky coach

I never realized there was such a difference between making a suggestion and making a decision.

— Dale Bandy, Ohio basketball coach, on the difference
between head coaches and assistant coaches

We get less publicity. We get less money. But we are equal in getting high blood pressure, ulcers, heart attacks and, oh yes, fired.

— Torchy Clark, Division II college basketball coach,
comparing coaching at Division I

Tommy's the only manager in the major leagues who uses a fork for a letter opener.

— Rick Monday, Los Angeles Dodgers outfielder, on Dodgers
manager Tom Lasorda

Tommy's amazing. Why, he'll even talk to numbers on an elevator. When they're lit up, he thinks they're listening.

> — *Don Sutton, Los Angeles Dodgers pitcher, on Tom Lasorda*

I know my players don't like my practices, but then, I don't like their games.

> — *Harry Neale, Vancouver Canucks coach, in the midst of a losing streak*

Doctors bury their mistakes. We still have ours on scholarship.

> — *Abe Lemons, University of Texas basketball coach*

The toughest thing for me as a young manager is that a lot of my players saw me play. They know how bad I was.

> — *Tony La Russa, Chicago White Sox manager*

They say most good managers were mediocre players. I should be a helluva manager.

> — *Charlie Hough, Texas Rangers pitcher*

It's a lot tougher to be a football coach than a President. You've got four years as a President, and they guard you. A coach doesn't have anyone to protect him when things go wrong.

> — *Harry S. Truman, thirty-third President of the United States*

I told my players "Watch the fake," and that's what they did. They watched the fake.

> — *John Durham, high school football coach, on a two-point conversion*

The time-outs smell a lot better.

> — *Butch Van Breda Kolff, basketball coach, why he likes his job with a woman's basketball league*

My players can wear their hair as long as they want and dress anyway they want. That is if they can pay their own tuition, meals and board.

> *— Eddie Robinson, Grambling University football coach*

Ben, there are a lot of bruisers who may come after you, but just remember this...the bigger they are, the harder they hit.

> *— Ben Agajanian, NY Giants football team kicker,*
> *receiving advice from his coach*
> *on how to keep from being hurt*

You're the only group of people who get more advice on how to run your business than we elected officials do.

> *— John Connally, Texas governor,*
> *speaking to a group of high school coaches*

I told my players to hold their hands as high as possible and spread their fingers wider apart to get more reach. So Oscar shot between their fingers.

> *— Red Auerbach, Boston Celtics coach, on his advice on how*
> *to keep Oscar Robertson from scoring*

I wouldn't do anything except polish his shot for him.

> *— Jack Patterson, Texas track coach, on how he*
> *would coach shot-putter Randy Matson*

You listen to the ball and bat coming together. They make an awful noise.

> *— Darrell Johnson, Seattle Mariners baseball manager,*
> *on when he knows to take a pitcher out of the game*

Well, coaching is like a bath. If you stay in long enough, it's not so hot.

> *— Biggie Munn, Michigan State athletic director,*
> *when asked if he missed coaching football*

Stay here a little bit longer so they'll think we know what the hell we're doing.

> *— John Ralston, Denver Broncos football coach,*
> *asking his quarterback not to return to his huddle*

Whoever answers the bullpen phone.

> — *Chuck Estrada, last place Texas Rangers pitching coach, on how he decides who relieves*

Coaching is like riding a motorcycle. The longer you do it, the more apt you are to get killed.

> — *Bill Fitch, Houston Rockets coach*

My college pitching coach taught me to pitch with 3 C's—Confidence, Control and Poise. That's the catch. You're thinking 3 C's and there are only 2 and that poise makes you think twice as hard.

> — *Steve Dunning, Cleveland Indians pitcher*

All those college football coaches who hold dressing room prayers before a game should be forced to attend church once a week.

> — *Duffy Daugherty, Michigan State football coach*

I give the same half-time speech over and over. It works best when my players are better than the other coach's players.

> — *Chuck Mills, Wake Forest football coach*

A life of frustration is inevitable for any coach whose main enjoyment is winning.

> — *Chuck Knoll, Pittsburgh Steelers coach*

A manager is like a fellow swimming in the ocean with a cut on his arm. Sooner or later the sharks are going to get him.

> — *Eddie Stanky, Texas Rangers manager*

Owners

Baseball owners have moral scruples against taking any man's dollar when there is a chance to take a dollar and a quarter.

> — *Red Smith, sportswriter*

We had a common bond on the A's: everybody hated Charlie Finley.

> — *Reggie Jackson, New York Yankees outfielder*
> *after being traded from Oakland*

It was a beautiful thing to behold, with all thirty-six oars working in unison.

> — *Jack Buck, sportscaster, on New York Yankees owner George*
> *Steinbrenner's new yacht*

He's the kind of guy Dale Carnegie would like to punch in the mouth.

> — *Bill Veeck, Chicago White Sox owner,*
> *on Walter O'Malley, Los Angeles Dodgers owner*

Finley is a self-made man who worships his creator.

> — *Jim Murray, Los Angeles Times*

I tell George what I think and then I do what he says.

> — *Bob Lemon, New York Yankees manager,*
> *on his boss, George Steinbrenner*

Being around him made me feel well.

> — *Jimmy Piersall, Boston Red Sox outfielder and former*
> *mental patient, on Oakland A's owner Charles O. Finley*

He's the kind of guy who would steal your eyes and then try to convince you that you looked better without them.

> — *Sam Rutigliano, Cleveland Browns coach,*
> *on Al Davis, Oakland Raiders owner*

We're 28 Republicans who vote socialist.

> — *Art Modell, Cleveland Browns owner, on NFL owners*

It's a good thing Babe Ruth still isn't here. If he was, George [Steinbrenner] would have him bat seventh and say he's overweight.

> — *Graig Nettles, New York Yankees infielder*

He should stick to horses. At least he can shoot them if they spit the bit.

> — *Reggie Jackson, California Angels outfielder,*
> *on former boss George Steinbrenner*

I could go out and buy 200,000 acres of timberland, but then what would I do? Cheer for the trees?

> — *David McConnell, wealthy New Yorker,*
> *on buying a NFL franchise in New Orleans*

Finley is so cold-blooded, he ought to make anti-freeze commercials.

> — *Reggie Jackson, New York Yankees outfielder*

We're interested, but Barron Hilton's price isn't exactly right. We only want to buy the San Diego Chargers football team, not the hotels.

> — *Bob Hope, comedian*

I got three years left on my present contract and by then all the owners may be broke.

> — *George Brett, Kansas City Royals,*
> *on the large contracts of superstars*

George Steinbrenner talks out of both sides of his wallet.

> — *Ron Luciano, major league umpire*

I'd sell them.

> — *Bill Veeck, former Cleveland Indians owner,*
> *on what he would do if he owned them once more*

I'm going to write a book about my days with Finley. I'm going to call it, *And They Thought I Was Crazy.*

> — *Jimmy Piersall, former Boston Red Sox outfielder*

National League owners are 100% for progress and 100% against change. I think it was a long time before any of them had inside plumbing.

> — *Edward Bennett Williams, Baltimore Orioles owner*

Sure, all summer.

> — *Joe Robbie, Miami Dolphins owner,*
> *if he would give his new coach, Don Shula,*
> *time to develop a winning team*

I get a feeling that the players think the energy crisis means them, so they only give 85%.

> — *Tad Potter, owner of the inept Pittsburgh Penquins*

When Charlie Finley had his heart operation, it took eight hours—seven just to find his heart.

> — *Steve McCatty, Oakland A's pitcher*

If you'll excuse us, we all have planes to catch to various courts around the country.

> — *Bowie Kuhn, baseball commissioner,*
> *closing a meeting of owners*

Those other owners, they're all egotists. They've got so much money. But nobody knew who they were before baseball. Who the hell ever heard of Ted Turner or Ray Kroc or George Steinbrenner?

> — *Calvin Griffith, Minnesota Twins owner*

Some of the owners in baseball, if they had a brain, would be idiots.

> — *Charlie Finley, Oakland Athletics, owner*

OFFICIALS

Umpiring is best described as the profession of standing between two seven year olds with one ice cream cone.

> — *Ron Luciano, major league umpire,*
> The Umpire Strikes Back

Umpiring's tough; you're always half wrong.

> — *Bill White, sportscaster and former*
> *Philadelphia Phillies infielder*

I occasionally get birthday cards from fans, but it's often the same message: they hope it's my last.

> — *Al Forman, major league umpire*

Why is it that they boo me when I call a foul ball correctly and they applaud the starting pitcher when he gets taken out of the ballgame?

> — *Jerry Neudecker, major league umpire*

When I'm right, no one remembers. When I'm wrong, no one forgets.

> — *Doug Harvey, major league umpire*

The president of the league is the only guy who comes to the ballgame and roots for the umpire.

> — *Hank Greenwald, San Francisco Giants announcer*

Many fans look upon an umpire as a sort of necessary evil to the luxury of baseball, like the odor that follows an automobile.

> — *Christy Mathewson, former New York Giants pitcher*

They expect an umpire to be perfect on opening day and to improve as the season goes on.

> — *Nestor Chylak, major league umpire*

Umpires are most vigorous when defending their miscalls.

> — *Jim Brosnan, Chicago Cubs pitcher*

Umpires sleep with their eyes open.

> — *Lon Simmons, Oakland A's announcer*

Nobody ever says anything nice about an umpire, unless it's when he dies and then somebody writes in the paper, "He was a good umpire." Oh, once in a while a player will tell you that you worked a good game behind the plate, but when that happens, it's always the winning pitcher who says it.

> — *Tom Gorman, major league umpire*

It's wonderful to be here, to be able to hear the baseball against the bat, ball against glove, and be able to boo the umpire.

> — *General Douglas MacArthur*

It's nothin' till I call it.

> — *Bill Klem, major league umpire*

When in doubt, call 'em out!

> — *Ron Luciano, Strike Two*

Call 'em fast and walk away tough.

> — *Tim Hurst, major league umpire*

If a manager covers home plate with dirt and you clean it while he is within kicking distance, he will cover it again. Every time you clean it, he will cover it. Do not clean it until he is safely in the dugout, preferably in the clubhouse.

> — *Ron Luciano, Strike Two*

You argue with the umpire because there's nothing else you can do about it.

> — *Leo Durocher, Brooklyn Dodgers manager*

Now, what the hell. Do you think I'd admit it?

> — *Augie Donatelli, major league umpire,*
> *asked if he ever made a bad call*

I don't count 'em, I just call 'em.

> — *Earl Strom, NBA official, answering a complaint*
> *that he had called too many fouls on one team*

I've been mobbed, cussed, booed, kicked in the ass, punched in the face, hit with mud balls and whiskey bottles, and had everything from shoes to fruits and vegetables thrown at me. An umpire should hate humanity.

> — *Joe Rue, major league umpire*

The old fans used to yell, "Kill the umpire!" The new fan tries to do it.

> — *Dr. Arnold Beisser, psychiatrist*

This must be the only job in America that everybody knows how to do better than the guy who's doing it.

> — *Nestor Chylak, major league umpire*

We have the best officials in all sports—you don't see them until you need them.

> — *Jerry Pate, professional golfer*

When I retire, I'm going to get a pair of gray slacks, a white shirt, a striped tie, a blue blazer, a case of dandruff and go stand on the first tee so I can be a USGA official.

> — *Lee Trevino, professional golfer*

You can say something to popes, kings, and presidents. But you can't talk to officials. In the next war, they ought to give everybody a whistle.

> — *Abe Lemons, University of Texas*
> *basketball coach*

Officiating is the only occupation in the world where the highest accolade is silence.

> — *Earl Strom, NBA referee*

The only thing tougher than being a basketball referee is being happily married.

> — *Skip Caray, sportscaster*

During the week I practice law. On Sundays I am the law.
> — *Tommy Bell, NFL official and attorney*

Major league pitchers are perhaps the most blessed people in the world. Not only are they born with super arms, able to throw a baseball harder and with some movement to the same location 85 to 110 times every four days, they are also born with super eyesight that enables them to see better from sixty feet six inches than an umpire can see from only three or four feet.

> — *Ron Luciano,* The Umpire Strikes Back

Plenty of players will like that.

> — *Joe West, major league umpire,*
> *playing in a movie where he gets shot*

Being an umpire is like being a king. It prepares you for nothing.

> — *Ron Luciano, former umpire*

Trying to convince an official they're wrong is like trying to convince your wife you're right.

> — *Dennis Harrah, Los Angeles Rams football player,*
> *on NFL officials*

We're not allowed to comment on the lousy officiating.

> — *Jim Finks, New Orleans Saints general manager,*
> *on the officiating of a game they lost*

I can see the sun, and it's 93 million miles away.

> — *Bruce Froemming, major league umpire,*
> *when fans needled him on his eyesight*

What would they do with chest protectors? Rebuild them?

> — *Early Wynn, Cleveland Indians pitcher,*
> *on women umpires*

The officials called fouls like they were getting a commision.

> — *Peter Salzburg, Vermont University basketball coach, when*
> *his team had committed 56 fouls*

If you painted our soccer balls orange and threw one to a linesman, he'd probably try to peel it.

> — *Jimmy Gabriel, Seattle Sounders soccer coach,*
> *on officials*

I liked the officials. They couldn't understand a word I was saying.

> — *Lefty Driesell, University of Maryland basketball coach,*
> *after his team returned from playing in Mexico City*

In all my years as an umpire, I've never had a person come up to me and say, "Are you Nestor Chylak, the umpire?"

> — *Nestor Chylak, major league umpire*

If they did get a machine to replace us, you know what would happen to it? Why, the players would bust it to pieces every time it ruled against them. They'd clobber it with a bat.

> — *Harry Wendelstedt, major league umpire*

THE COMMISSIONER

Bowie is the best commissioner in baseball today.

> — *Jim Bouton, New York Yankees pitcher,*
> *on Bowie Kuhn, commissioner of baseball*

I have often called Bowie Kuhn a village idiot. I apologize to the village idiots of America. He is the nation's idiot.

> — *Charles O. Finley, Oakland A's owner*

His career typifies the heights to which dramatic talent can carry a man in America, if only he has the foresight not to go on the stage.

> — *Heywood Broun, sportswriter, on Judge Kenesaw Mountain Landis, baseball commissioner*

We had a meeting with Lee MacPhail, league president, and he told us we liked it.

> — *Chuck Tanner, Chicago White Sox manager,*
> *if he liked the designated hitter rule*

I've got to remind myself that I'm the only guy in the park who is there to root for the umpire.

> — *Chub Feeny, National League president*

One wonders whether the baseball commissioner received the designation because the Bible starts with the words, "In the big inning."

> — *A fan, on Bowie Kuhn being named*
> *chairman of National Bible Week*

THE PRESS

If I ever need a brain transplant, I want one from a sportswriter, because I'll know it's never been used.

> — *Joe Paterno, Penn State University football coach*

The best three years of a sportswriter's life are the third grade.

> — *George Raveling, Washington State University basketball coach*

The Lord taught me to love everybody, but the last ones I learned to love were the sportswriters.

> — *Alvin Dark, Oakland A's manager*

All of us learn to write by the second grade, then most of us go on to other things.

> — *Bob Knight, Indiana University basketball coach*

Pour hot water over a sportswriter and you'll get instant bleep.

> — *Ted Williams, Boston Red Sox outfielder*

In Czechoslovakia there is no such thing as freedom of the press. In the United States there is no such thing as freedom from the press.

> — *Martina Navratilova, professional tennis player*

Absolute silence—that's the one thing a sportswriter can quote accurately.

> — *Bob Knight, Indiana University basketball coach*

I can remember a reporter asking for a quote, and I didn't know what a quote was. I thought it was some kind of soft drink.

> — *Joe Di Maggio, New York Yankees outfielder*

New York sportswriters are busy getting ready for the baseball season. They're going through their thesauruses looking for synonyms for "dictatorial," "obnoxious" and "eliminated."

> — *David Letterman, talk show host*

San Francisco writers describe the baseball scene with all the precision of three-year-old children fingerpainting on the playroom wall.

> — *Jim Brosnan,* The Long Season

Any sportswriter who thinks the world is no bigger than the outfield fence is not only a bad citizen of the world but also a lousy sportswriter.

> — *Red Smith, sportswriter*

My wife calls me Much-Maligned. She thinks that's my first name. Every time she reads a story about me, that's always in front of my name.

> — *Chris Bahr, Los Angeles Raiders kicker*

It has often occurred to me that sport, like sex, is an activity that should either be performed or watched—but not written about.

> — *Paul Gardner, writer*

I once thought of becoming a political cartoonist because they only have to come up with one idea a day. Then I thought I'd become a sportswriter instead, because they don't have to come up with any.

> — *Sam Snead, professional golfer*

To hell with newspapermen. You can buy them with a steak.

> — *George Weiss, New York Yankees executive*

I don't think I've been asked this many questions since my mother caught me drinking in high school.

> — *Don Strock, Miami Dolphins, after reporters*
> *beseiged him when he replaced Dan Marino*

If you don't think you're out, read the morning paper.

> — *Bill McGowan, retired umpire,*
> *when a player argued that he wasn't out*

I notice they take a thousand pictures of me, but the papers always use the ones in which I'm not smiling.

> — *Roger Maris, NY Yankees outfielder,*
> *who had trouble with the NY press*

You guys would stick that equipment in a coffin.

> — *Vince Lombardi, Washington Redskins coach,*
> *when a TV crew butted in on a conversation*
> *with his quarterback*

I'm going to write a letter to the President. If the Soviets want a journalist, I've got about a hundred of the S.O.B.'s. I'd like to give 'em.

> — *Bob Knight, Indiana basketball coach, when*
> *the Russians held journalist Nicholas Daniloff*

It only proves that sportswriters indulge in more drugs than athletes do.

> — *Paul Evans, Pittsburgh basketball coach, when they*
> *were ranked in the top 20, in a preseason poll*

One of them has me dead, already.

> — *Mark Koenig, 1977 NY Yankees shortstop,*
> *on his dislike for books about the Yankees*

BASEBALL
Diamonds are Forever — and Ever

Next to religion, baseball has had a greater impact on the American people than any other institution.

> — *Herbert Hoover, thirty-first President of the United States*

Baseball is one of the arts.

> — *Ted Williams, Boston Red Sox outfielder*

Baseball is almost the only orderly thing in a very unorderly world. If you get three strikes, even the best lawyer in the world can't get you off.

> — *Bill Veeck, owner*

Whoever would understand the heart and mind of America had better learn baseball.

> — *Jacques Barzun, writer*

More than any other American sport, baseball creates the magnetic, addictive illusion that it can almost be understood.

> — *Thomas Boswell,* Inside Sports

Ninety feet between bases is the nearest to perfection that man has yet achieved.

> — *Red Smith, sportswriter*

You gotta be a man to play baseball for a living, but you gotta have a lot of little boy in you, too.

> — *Roy Campanella, Brooklyn Dodgers catcher*

Let's play two!

> — *Ernie Banks, Chicago Cubs infielder*

The Human Side

PRAISE

Joe Louis was a newspaperman's champion. He always finished in time for the first edition so us guys could get our stories done and make it to the bar with hours to go before closing time.

> — *Red Smith, sportswriter*

If Bear tells me it's raining, I don't look out to see. I go get an umbrella.

> — *Field Scovell, on Bear Bryant's image*

I'm probably the only guy who worked for Stengel before and after he became a genius.

> — *Warren Spahn, pitching great, on Casey Stengel*

Tell Len I'm proud of him. I hope he does better next time.

> — *Tokie Lockhart, Len Barker's grandmother,*
> *after he pitched a perfect game*

Harmon Killebrew could hit the ball out of any park in the country, and that includes Yellowstone.

> — *Paul Richards, Baltimore Orioles manager*

He can play all three outfield positions—at the same time.

> — *Gene Mauch, Philadelphia Phillies manager,*
> *on Cesar Cedeno, Houston Astros outfielder*

 The earth is two-thirds covered by water. The other third is covered by Gary Maddox.

> — *Ralph Kiner, Pittsburgh Pirates outfielder*
> *turned sportscaster*

He had larceny in his heart, but his feet were honest.

> — *Arthur "Bugs" Baer, sportswriter,*
> *on Ping Bodie, New York Yankees outfielder*

Give him the ball.

> — *Magic Johnson, Los Angeles Lakers, on what he had learned after playing with Kareem Abdul-Jabbar*

You might as well put a cape on him.

> — *Elvis Patterson, cornerback, on John Elway's super moves*

Going into a game against Lew Alcindor is like going into a knife fight and finding there's no blade in your handle.

> — *Bill Fitch, Cleveland Cavaliers coach*

Man, what could he get if he could shoot free throws!

> — *Oscar Robertson, Cincinnati Royals basketball star, on Wilt Chamberlain receiving a large contract*

He's the greatest living shortstop of all times.

> — *Paul Richards, Baltimore Orioles manager, on Chicago's Lou Aparicio*

He's the only guy I know who can go four for three.

> — *Alan Bannister, Chicago White Sox infielder, on Rod Carew*

Giving Magic the basketball is like giving Hitler an army, Jesse James a gang, or Genghis Khan a horse. Devastation. Havoc.

> — *Jim Murray, sportswriter, LA Times*

I would be willing to go to jail six months to have him. I'd gladly go on bread and water and relish every bite and every sip.

> — *Terry Crisp, Calgary Flames coach, on what he thought of Mario Lemieux*

Nobody ever rode a horse with the skill and grace of Bill Shoemaker. The worst rogues on the track turned into swans when he got on them. It wasn't a race, it was a romance. A love affair. Shoe didn't ride a horse, he joined him. Most riders treat horses as if they were guards in slave-labor camps. Shoe treated them as if he were asking them to dance.

— Jim Murray, sportswriter, LA Times

We finally got Nebraska where we want them...off the schedule.

— Cal Stoll, Minnesota football coach

The last time anybody jumped like that in Chicago was when Mayor Daley asked an alderman to get him a cup of coffee.

— Mike Downey, Chicago Daily News,
on David Thompson

He's quick enough to play tennis by himself.

— Jim Killingsworth, TCU basketball coach,
on Tulsa player Paul Pressey

BRAGGING

This man had an illustrious high school career, an illustrious college career and an illustrious career in the pros. But enough about me.

> — *John Kerr, Chicago Bulls announcer, when he introduced Julius Erving*

When I told my doctor I was marrying a 33-year old woman, he said I could be taking a chance. I told him, "Hey, if she dies, she dies."

> — *Willie Pep, ex-fighter, when he was 65 years old*

Women can't play a lick. I'll prove that. I'll set women's tennis back twenty years.

> — *Bobby Riggs, professional tennis player*

Young man, you have the question backwards.

> — *Bill Russell, sportscaster and former Boston Celtics center, when asked how he would have fared, playing against Kareem Abdul-Jabbar*

My greatest strength is that I have no weaknesses.

> — *John McEnroe, professional tennis player*

I'm the straw that stirs the drink.

> — *Reggie Jackson, New York Yankees outfielder*

If I were playing in New York, they'd name a candy bar after me.

> — *Reggie Jackson, Oakland A's outfielder*

I was such a dangerous hitter I even got intentional walks in batting practice.

> — *Casey Stengel, New York Yankees manager*

Hell, I could've hit .600 myself, but I'm paid to hit homers.

— Babe Ruth, New York Yankees outfielder, to Ty Cobb

You've got to remember, the man is 73 years old.

— Sportswriter, c. 1960, when asked what Ty Cobb would hit against modern pitching if he were still playing, and defending his answer that he'd hit only about .300

I'd pay to see me play.

— Elvin Hayes, Washington Bullets forward

People say my ego is grand. I think it's in proportion to me.

— Wilt Chamberlain, former NBA center

All I know is I've won every award there is to win in this game except comeback player of the year—which I'll get next year.

— Pete Rose, Philadelphia Phillies infielder, after a bad season

I could nip frosting off a cake with my fastball.

— Satchel Paige, Negro Leagues pitcher

I'm going to win so much this year that my caddie will make the top twenty money winners list.

— Lee Trevino, professional golfer

When you're as great as I am, it's hard to be humble.

— Muhammad Ali, heavyweight champion

Me, on instant replay.

— Derek Sanderson, Boston Bruins center, when asked to name the greatest hockey player he ever saw

My only regret in life is that I can't sit up in the stands and watch me pitch.

> — *Bo Belinsky, Los Angeles Angels pitcher*

The only reason I don't like playing in the World Series is I can't watch myself play.

> — *Reggie Jackson, New York Yankees outfielder*

I know I'm getting better at golf because I'm hitting fewer spectators.

> — *Gerald R. Ford, amateur golfer*

Sometimes I amaze even myself.

> — *Reggie Jackson, New York Yankees outfielder*

Two thing's for sure: the sun's gonna shine and I'm going three for four.

> — *Dave Parker, Pittsburgh Pirates outfielder*

Death, taxes and my jump shot.

> — *Otis Birdsong, New Jersey Nets guard,*
> *on the three immutables of life*

No, why should I?

> — *Don Larsen, New York Yankees pitcher,*
> *asked if he ever tires of talking about his perfect game*
> *in the 1956 World Series*

I don't compare them, I just catch them.

> — *Willie Mays, New York Giants outfielder,*
> *when asked to cite his greatest catch*

The baseline belongs to me.

> — *Ty Cobb, Detroit Tigers outfielder*

I can say with a clear conscience that I have never knowingly bit another football player. For one thing, I believe in good hygiene.

> — *Conrad Dobler, St. Louis Cardinals lineman*

I do believe that my best hits border on felonious assault.
> — *Jack Tatum, Oakland Raiders defensive back*

There's no such thing as bragging. You're either lying or telling the truth.
> — *Al Oliver, Pittsburgh Pirates outfielder*

It ain't braggin' if you can do it.
> — *Dizzy Dean, St. Louis Cardinals pitcher*

He reminds me of a young me.
> — *World B. Free, Cleveland Cavaliers guard,*
> *on rookie Jeff Malone*

Is he cocky? If Cocky met Pete Incaviglia he'd blush.
> — *Paul Daugherty, Newsday writer,*
> *on baseball player, Incaviglia*

Empty barrels make the most noise.
> — *Chuck Noll, Pittsburgh Steelers football coach,*
> *about a player who brags a great deal*

I told all the guys before the contest who was going to win. I just wanted to know who was to come in second.
> — *Larry Bird, Boston Celtics basketball star,*
> *on the three point shooting contest*

I am the best golfer. I just haven't played yet.
> — *Cassius Clay, heavyweight boxer*

It couldn't happen to a greater guy. Well yes, it could have happened to me.
> — *Tommy Lasorda, after Jerry Reuss pitched a no-hitter*

Here the Joneses try to keep up with the Holmeses.

> — *Larry Holmes, heavyweight champ,*
> *on why he still lives in Easton, PA*

If Satch and I were pitching on the same team, we'd clinch the pennant by July 4th and go fishing until World Series time.

> — *Dizzy Dean*

In modern society, one earns what one is worth.

> — *Helenio Herrera, Italian soccer coach,*
> *commenting on the fact that his salary*
> *is ten times that of the minister of government*

Arnold is the greatest putter in the world. He's better than I am—and I'm the best.

> — *Lee Trevino, golfer, on why he is considering*
> *promoting a young golfer, Arnold Salines*

I used to watch Michigan play on TV and they were so terrible I knew they really needed help.

> — *Cazzie Russell, basketball player,*
> *explaining how he chose his school*

Tell me where he's at. I will buy his town and have him deported.

> — *Muhammad Ali, when told that an Amish*
> *man had never heard of him*

I'm all for women's lib. They should all have equal opportunity with me.

> — *Jerry LeVais, pro football player*

I am the greatest.

> — *Muhammad Ali, heavyweight champion*

SELF CONFIDENCE

This plane isn't going to crash. I'm on it.
> — *Muhammad Ali, to a passenger on a bouncy air flight*

Serenity is knowing that your worst shot is still going to be pretty good.
> — *Johnny Miller, pro golfer*

One thing I do suffer from is over-confidence. It's something I'm working on.
> — *George Foreman, boxer*

If you travel first-class, you think first-class and you're more likely to play first-class.
> — *Ray Floyd, pro golfer, who is a big spender*

He's the only person I know who bought a plane before he learned to fly.
> — *Rocky Blier, Pittsburgh Steelers,*
> *on coach Chuck Noll's self-confidence*

When I went duck hunting with Bear Bryant, he shot at one, but it kept flying. "John," he said, "there flies a dead duck." Now that's confidence.
> — *John McKay, University of Southern*
> *California football coach*

BEING HUMAN

We could have stopped him if he was human.

> — *Doug Collins, Chicago Bulls basketball coach, on trying to stop Larry Bird*

I never noticed that Bird was black or white. I didn't even know he was human.

> — *Frank Layden, Utah Jazz coach, on comments made by Isiah Thomas against Larry Bird*

Sure, such tests are dehumanizing. But when you think about it, so is football.

> — *Doug English, Detroit Lions, on urine tests*

The Bear's always been ahead of us humans. Even when we started the two-platoon system, he was using three platoons: one on offense, one on defense and one to go to class.

> — *Frank Howard, Clemson football coach, about Bear Bryant*

# HUMILITY

I always thought that was an honor for guys who could see without glasses and eat corn with their own teeth.

— Jim Murray, sports columnist,
when inducted into the Hall of Fame

The big milestone in anybody's career is when Tom Landry calls you by your first name. The first time it happened to me, I almost changed my name to what he called me—Ray.

— Bill MacAtee, ex-Dallas Cowboy

Earl Campbell ain't like those high-priced, spoiled athletes. Why, he had me over to his office the other day just like one of the guys.

— Bum Phillips, Houston Oilers coach

I don't think anybody in the world wants to be zero and anything, let alone zero and 13. This has given me a tremendous amount of humility. I was always humble, but now I'm overly humble.

— Ray Robbins, Philadelphia 76ers, after a losing streak

I had to adjust when I came to UCLA. When I played well, we won. When I was mediocre, we won. And when I played badly, we won.

— Greg Lee, former UCLA basketball player

SELF-KNOCKS

I usually don't give a good first impression, or a second impression. For that matter I usually come across like a sack of manure.

> — *Doug Rader, Texas Rangers manager*

You ought to see my mail. I didn't know there were so many ways to call somebody stupid.

> — *Ray Knight, Baltimore Orioles baseball player,*
> *after rejecting a larger offer to play for the NY Mets*

Wherever I go, people are waving at me. Maybe if I do a good job, they'll use all their fingers.

> — *Frank King, Winter Olympic Games*
> *organizing committee chairman*

You know, it used to take 43 Marv Throneberry cards to get one Carl Furillo.

> — *Marv Throneberry, former NY Mets first baseman*

My career has been pretty checkered. This might be checkmate.

> — *Ken Dunek, defunct USFL's Baltimore Stars*

I'm glad I don't have a fourth pitch.

> — *Roger Mason, San Francisco Giants pitcher,*
> *after three consecutive homers*

I'm the greatest 60-foot pitcher in baseball. If I can conquer those last six inches, I'll be on my way.

> — *Barry Latman, Los Angeles Dodgers pitcher*

I'm doing it for the next coach. Think how easy it will be to follow me.

> — *Gomer Jones, on why he would be willing*
> *to be the football coach at Oklahoma,*
> *following the legendary Bud Wilkinson*

I'm going home and going straight to sleep. If I dream, I'll dream about shooting myself—but I'll probably miss.

> — *Xavier McDaniel, Seattle SuperSonics basketball player,*
> *after missing most of his baskets*

It's pretty bad when your family asks for passes to the game and want to sit in the left-field bleachers.

> — *Bert Blyleven, Minnesota Twins*
> *pitcher, noted for allowing many*
> *home runs*

I'm expecting a good season. I don't know why. Just ignorance, I guess.

> — *Abe Martin, TCU football coach,*
> *on the kind of season he expects*

A low IQ helps.

> — *Keith Lincoln, San Diego Chargers*
> *halfback, on why he played in an all-*
> *star game with an injured knee*

I was taught at an early age to get big scores and I can't change for the life of me.

> — *Harry Stuhldreher, former Notre Dame football great,*
> *on his golf game*

Distance is no problem, only direction. I might tee off on the first hole and wind up putting on the ninth.

> — *Al Feuerbach, shot-putter, on his golf game*

Sometimes I'm stranger than the truth.

> — *John Riggins, Washington Redskins, on looking*
> *at an old picture of himself with a Mohawk haircut*

The rest of the field.

> — *Roger Maltbie, pro golfer,*
> *on what he needs to shoot to win a tournament*

If we hadn't won I would have jumped off a tall building. But the way I'm hitting, I wouldn't have hit the ground anyway.

> — *Phil Garner, Los Angeles Dodgers,*
> *after he hit into a triple play*

I could play the pilot in a war film, who dropped his first bomb and it was incomplete.

> — *Don Meredith, former Dallas Cowboy quarterback,*
> *on his future as a movie star*

If the Cougars have one outstanding trait this season, it's mediocrity.

> — *Marv Harshman, Washington State basketball coach*

Nobody wants to miss it in case we ever win one.

> — *Joe Young, Tilburg, Ontario mayor, on why the*
> *local hockey team always played to a capacity crowd*

I would like to think my job is in jeopardy. It would show somebody is interested.

> — *Joe Gasparella, Carnegie-Mellon football coach*

We looked great against the dummies. Too bad we don't play Dummy University.

> — *Lou Holtz, Arkansas football coach*

We're so bad right now that for us, back-to-back home runs means one today and another one tomorrow.

> — *Earl Weaver, Baltimore Orioles manager*

I thought I did, until I looked at some old game films.

> — *Bum Phillips, Houston Oilers football coach,*
> *when asked if he ever played football*

My coaching.

> — *Dick Vermeil, Philadelphia Eagles coach,*
> *on what worried him most*

This winter I'm working out every day, throwing at a wall. I'm 11-0 against the wall.

> — *Jim Bouton, ex-major league pitcher,*
> *trying for a comeback*

There was nothing to lose.

> — *Ron Farley, 40-year old Angel, why he has not lost speed*

My fastball.

> — *Tommy John, if anything was missing*
> *after a burglary in the clubhouse*

It was so bad the players were giving each other high fives when they hit the rim.

> — *Ron Shumate, Southeast Missouri State basketball coach, on*
> *his weak team*

My IQ must be two points lower than a plant's.

> — *Tom Watson, pro golfer,*
> *disqualified for illegally changing putters*

When the year was over they wanted to give me back as the player to be named later.

> — *Richie Scheinblum, Cincinnati Reds outfielder, when he was*
> *traded for cash and a player to be named later*

NAME CALLING

When we win, he's Sweet Old Bob. When we lose, they just use the initials.

> — *Carl Selmer, Nebraska offensive line coach,*
> *on the fans' support of head coach, Bob Devaney*

How could he be doing his job when he didn't throw me out of the game after the things I called him?

> — *Mark Belanger, Baltimore Orioles, on umpire Russ Goetz*

Not while I'm alive.

> — *Irving Rudd, boxing publicist, when Howard Cosell said, "I am my own worst enemy."*

Tommy really has a one-track mind, and the traffic on it is very light. He's one guy who has a sixth sense, but there's no evidence of the other five.

> — *Steve Garvey, Los Angeles Dodgers first baseman,*
> *on manager Tommy Lasorda*

There's talk about this guy becoming a U.S. senator. When he becomes senator, I'm buying Russian war bonds.

> — *Tom Lasorda, Los Angeles Dodgers manager,*
> *on Steve Garvey*

When J.C. [Snead] was a kid, he was so ugly they had to tie a pork chop around his neck to get the dog to play with him.

> — *Lee Trevino, professional golfer*

The shoulder surgery was a success. The lobotomy failed.

> — *Mike Ditka, Chicago Bears coach,*
> *on Jim McMahon's surgery*

A robot, a solitary, mechanical man who lives with his dogs behind towering walls at his estate in Connecticut. A man who wants so badly to have a more human image that he's having surgery to remove the bolts from his neck.

> — *Tony Kornheiser, Washington Post columnist,*
> *on Ivan Lendl*

Everybody knows that Casey Stengel has forgotten more baseball than I'll ever know. But that's just the trouble — he's forgotten it.

> — *Jimmy Piersall, former Boston Red Sox outfielder*

How dumb can the hitters in this league get? I've been doing this for fifteen years. When they're batting with the count two balls and no strikes, or three and one, they're always looking for a fastball. And they never get it.

> — *Eppa Rixey, Cincinnati Reds pitcher*

We got a guy on our club who has such bad hands his glove is embarrassed.

> — *Frank Sullivan, Philadelphia Phillies pitcher*

Next to the catcher, the third baseman has to be the dumbest guy out there. You can't have any brains and take those shots all day.

> — *Dave Elder, Seattle Mariners infielder*

His best weapon is his chin.

> — *Richie Giachetti, fight manager,*
> *on former middleweight champ Vito Antuofermo*

Well, 35 million TV viewers know that Karras has a lot of class. And all of it is third.

> — *Conrad Dobler, pro football player,*
> *when Alex Karras called him a dirty player*

For me to fight a man like that and still face my conscience, I would have to agree to let him carry a pistol.

> — *Archie Moore, light-heavyweight champion,*
> *on a proposed bout with middleweight Paul Pender*

Bob [Hope] has a beautiful short game. Unfortunately, it's off the tee.

> — *Jimmy Demaret, professional golfer*

I'll tell you how smart Pete [Rose] is. When they had the blackout in New York, he was stranded 13 hours on an escalator.

> — *Joe Nuxhall, Cincinnati Reds broadcaster*

Play me or trade me.

> — *Don Zimmer (among many others),*
> *Brooklyn Dodgers infielder*

We played him, and now we can't trade him.

> — *Buzzy Bavasi, Brooklyn Dodgers general manager,*
> *on Don Zimmer*

Why are we honoring this man? Have we run out of human beings?

> — *Milton Berle, on Howard Cosell*

The Goose should do more pitching and less quacking.

> — *George Steinbrenner, New York Yankees owner,*
> *on Goose Gossage*

He's everything a good heavyweight should be, except busy.

> — *Rocky Marciano, boxer, on Floyd Patterson*

Well, maybe he could have gone another 15, but he wouldn't have went them with me.

> — *Ray Robinson, boxer, when Carmen Basillio*
> *said he could go another 15 rounds*

If he's the people's champion, then asparagus is the people's vegetable.

> — *Bernie Linicome, Chicago Tribune writer,*
> *after Larry Holmes called himself the people's*
> *champion*

Today I told my little girl I was going to the ballpark and she asked me, "What for?"

> — *Dave Anderson, seldom-used*
> *Los Angeles Dodgers infielder*

What's the Roman Numeral for zero?

> — *Jim Murray, Los Angeles Times columnist,*
> *on how many points the New England Patriots*
> *would score in the Super Bowl*

Some people throw to spots, some people throw to zones. Renie throws to zip codes.

> — *Dan Quisenberry, Kansas City Royals pitcher,*
> *on teammate Renie Martin*

To paraphrase Churchill, probably never has so little been done with so much.

> — *Bob Knight, Indiana basketball coach,*
> *on Louisiana State coach Dale Brown's coaching*

There would be a lot of offensive linemen playing indoor soccer next year.

> — *Bob Golic, Cleveland Browns football player,*
> *on clamping down on use of steroids*

You could put the brains of three of those guys in a hummingbird and it would still fly backwards.

> — *Fred Taylor, Ohio State University basketball coach,*
> *referring to his players*

He doesn't have ulcers, but he's a carrier.

> — *Jerry Kramer, Green Bay Packers football player,*
> *on Vince Lombardi*

He talks very well for a guy who's had two fingers in his mouth all his life.

> — *Gene Mauch, on Don Drysdale's announcing skills*

If it's true we learn by our mistakes, then Jim Frey will be the best manager ever.

> — *Ron Luciano, former major league umpire*

There is nothing quite so limited as being a limited partner of George Steinbrenner's.

> — *John McMullen, former partner of the Yankees*

You talk about being recycled. Don Zimmer is the aluminum can of managing.

> — *Tony Kornheiser, Washington Post,*
> *when Don Zimmer got his fourth managership*

His voice could peel the skin off of a potato.

> — *Norman Chad, Washington Post writer,*
> *on announcer Dick Vitale*

They had no class. They not only didn't take any of my boxing pictures hanging on the wall, they turned them around.

> — *Art Aragon, former boxer,*
> *after his home had been robbed*

With that dinky slider, he's so bad, he's the only batting practice pitcher who can get people into slumps.

> — *Charlie Smith, NY Mets third baseman,*
> *on Yogi Berra as a batting practice pitcher*

Who shot the couch?

> — *Frank Glieber, CBS,*
> *when he saw Billy Packer in an unusual sports coat*

He's spent several years in the majors plus several more with the Pirates.

> — *Don Mattingly, NY Yankees,*
> *on newly acquired veteran Rick Rhoden*

I'm not used to being funny and cracking jokes like everyone else is doing. In Cleveland we took our banquets seriously and saved the jokes for our games.

> — *Von Hayes, at a banquet, after being traded*
> *to Philadelphia from Cleveland*

Since then we've changed the locks.

> — *James McNulty, Scranton mayor, after fight promoter*
> *Don King was given the key to the city*

Not if I have to have his brain, too.

> — *Bob Ojeda, New York Mets pitcher,*
> *when asked if he would like to have Ron Myers' fastball*

The safest place would be in the fairway.

> — *Joe Garagiola, on where the fans should stand*
> *in a celebrity golf tournament*

What's that, a Mr. T starter set?

> — *Mike Diaz, Pittsburgh Pirates baseball player,*
> *when he saw a young player wearing three gold chains*

No, something much simpler, journalism.

> — *Tom Cousineau, San Francisco 49ers linebacker, responding*
> *to a reporter's questioning if he studied basket-weaving in*
> *college*

Sparky came here two years ago promising to build a team in his own image, and now the club is looking for small white-haired infielders with .212 batting averages.

> — *Al Ackerman, Detroit Tigers announcer,*
> *on Sparky Anderson, manager of the Tigers*

We're just two or three pitchers away from being a fourth-place club.

> — *Ray Nock, Cleveland fan*

Football coaches walk across the field after the game and pretend to congratulate the opposing coach. Baseball managers head right for the beer.

> — *Thomas Boswell, Washington Post*
> *columnist*

I have tried very hard to like Howard. And I have failed.

> — *Red Smith, columnist, on Howard*
> *Cosell*

Look, why don't we talk about this when you pick up my trash on Monday.

> — *Sean Farrell, Tampa Buccaneers guard,*
> *being annoyed by a spectator*

Neal Heaton is left-handed and nearly 27. As Casey Stengel might have said, "In 10 years, he has a chance to be left-handed and nearly 37."

> — *Marty Noble, Newsday writer, on a Montreal pitcher*

If I tried to put a finger on all of New Orleans' problems, I'd need five or six pairs of hands.

> — *Chuck Muncie, after being traded from New Orleans*

He showed us he could hit three ways: left, right and seldom.

> — *Joe Klein, Texas Rangers general manager,*
> *on Charley Pride, country singer,*
> *playing in an exhibition game and striking out twice*

Without him we're an average team. In fact, with him we're an average team.

> — *Gene Shue, Washington Bullets coach,*
> *on center Jeff Ruland*

Hubie was to network basketball ratings what the Titanic was to the winter cruise business.

> — *Pat Williams, Orlando Magic general manager,*
> *presenting NBA announcer Hubie Brown*

I sure hope I find one. When the season starts I'll be too busy helping the referees to play the position myself.

> *— Bones McKinney, Carolina Cougars basketball coach,*
> *on looking for a center*

Bobby Knight is a very good friend of mine. But, if I ever needed a heart transplant, I'd want his. It's never been used.

> *— George Raveling, USC basketball coach*

I'm glad it happened in front of the library. I've always emphasized scholarship.

> *— Doug Weaver, Kansas coach,*
> *on being hung in effigy in front of the library*

If you prefer baseball in slow motion, don't miss George Foster chasing a double into the left-field corner.

> *— Charles Bricker, sportswriter*

Lady, the woman in this house lets me sleep with her.

> *— Lee Trevino, golf pro, responding to a woman*
> *who wanted to know how much he charged to*
> *wash windows, after seeing him washing the*
> *windows of his house*

Because he's so full of it, he can't fly.

> *— Sparky Anderson, Detroit Tigers manager,*
> *on why he calls Tommy Lasorda "Walking Eagle"*

Most football players are temperamental. That's 90% temper and 10% mental.

> *— Doug Plank, former Chicago Bears football player*

That's pretty good, considering that Dave's previous idol was himself.

> *— Willie Stargell, retired baseball player,*
> *on Dave Parker's statement that Stargell was his idol*

So he won 800 games. Five hundred of them against Southeastern Conference teams. That's like me going to Texas with six kids from Canada and starting a hockey league.

> — *Johnny Dee, Notre Dame basketball coach,*
> *on legendary Adolph Rupp from Kentucky*

He's the guts of the Angels, our triple threat. He can hit, run and lob.

> — *Marv Rettenmund, California Angels coach,*
> *on Don Baylor*

Clemson will never subsidize a sport where a man sits on his tail and goes backwards.

> — *Frank Howard, Clemson athletic director, when*
> *asked to support scholarships for the rowing team*

You could send Inge Hammustion into the corner with six eggs in his pocket and he wouldn't break any of them.

> — *Harold Ballard, Toronto Maple Leafs owner,*
> *on his non-aggressive team*

He is self-effacing, modest, unassuming, bereft of ego, warm, gentle. But he makes up for it in incompetence.

> — *Harry Ornest, owner St. Louis Blues, on Norman Green*

Once you put it down, you can't pick it up. — It's chief fault is the covers are too far apart

> — *Pat Williams, NBA executive*
> *about Charles Barkley's autobiography*

BAD HABITS

My wife doesn't care what I do when I'm away, as long as I don't have a good time.

> — *Lee Trevino, professional golfer*

Bugs drank a lot, and sometimes it seemed like the more he drank the better he pitched. They used to say he didn't spit on the ball—he blew his breath on it, and the ball would come up drunk.

> — *Rube Marquard, New York Giants pitcher,*
> *on teammate Bugs Raymond*

Hell, if I didn't drink or smoke, I'd win twenty games every year. It's easy if you don't drink or smoke or horse around.

> — *Whitey Ford, New York Yankees pitcher*

If I were a Tibetan priest and ate everything perfect, maybe I'd live to be 105. The way I'm going now, I'll probably only make it to 102. I'll give away three years to beer.

> — *Bill Lee, Montreal Expos pitcher*

I have never led the tour in money winnings, but I have many times in alcohol consumption.

> — *Fuzzy Zoeller, professional golfer*

It depends on the length of the game.

> — *Mike "King" Kelly, Chicago Cubs outfielder,*
> *asked whether he drinks*
> *during a game*

If you drink, don't drive. Don't even putt.

> — *Dean Martin, entertainer*

You mix two jiggers of scotch and one jigger of Metrecal. So far I've lost five pounds and my driver's license.

> — *Rocky Bridges, Cincinnati Reds infielder,*
> *on his new diet*

I've never played drunk. Hungover, yes, but never drunk.

> — *Hack Wilson, Chicago Cubs outfielder*

If your doctor warns you that you have to watch your drinking, find a bar with a mirror.

> — *John Mooney, sportswriter*

It's a lot easier when you're starting because when you're starting you can pick your days to drink.

> — *Bill Lee, Boston Red Sox pitcher*

Mickey Mantle spilled more than I drank.

> — *Whitey Ford, former New York Yankees pitcher*

I asked Jimmy Demaret what was his favorite drink and he said, "The next one.

> — *Phil Harris, entertainer*

My handicaps are gin and old age.

> — *Mrs. Cecily Bishop, 71,*
> *dropped from a British golf tournament*

They say some of my stars drink whiskey, but I have found that the ones who drink milkshakes don't win many ballgames.

> — *Casey Stengel, New York Yankees manager*

We're in such a slump that even the ones that are drinkin' aren't hittin'.

> — *Casey Stengel, New York Yankees manager*

I deplored the cocaine, the marijuana and the other drugs. I used to stare across the line of scrimmage and see a linebacker sometimes where both eyes weren't going the same way.

> *— Roger Staubach, former Dallas Cowboys quarterback*

He doesn't know anything about drugs. He thinks uppers are dentures.

> *— Archie Griffin, former Ohio State running back,*
> *on coach Woody Hayes*

If cocaine were helium, the NBA would float away.

> *— Art Rust, sportscaster*

If the Food and Drug Administration ever walked into the Phils' clubhouse, they'd close down baseball.

> *— Tug McGraw, Philadelphia Phillies relief pitcher*

I don't know—I never smoked AstroTurf.

> *— Tug McGraw, Philadelphia Phillies pitcher,*
> *on whether he prefers grass or AstroTurf*

Amphetamines improved my performance about five percent. Unfortunately, in my particular case that wasn't enough.

> *— Jim Bouton, former New York Yankees pitcher*

I don't use steroids. I don't want to wake up some morning with a beard.

> *— Cheryl Miller, University of Southern*
> *California basketball player*

Going to bed with a woman never hurt a ballplayer. It's staying up all night looking for them that does you in.

> *— Casey Stengel, New York Yankees manager*

Y ou're gonna hit 50 homers and drive in 140 runs living a clean life. Why don't you just hit 40 and get 125 RBIs and mess around a little?

> — *Joe Morgan, Cincinnati Reds infielder,*
> *to teammate George Foster*

I f I hadn't met those two at the start of my career, I would have lasted another five years.

> — *Mickey Mantle, New York Yankees outfielder, on*
> *his off-field activities with Whitey Ford and Billy Martin*

I couldn't have pitched any better if I had lived in an iron lung and went to church twice on Sunday.

> — *Art Fowler, former California Angels pitcher*

W hen we won the league championship, all the married guys on the club had to thank their wives for putting up with all the stress and strain all season. I had to thank all the single broads in New York.

> — *Joe Namath, New York Jets quarterback*

Y ou gotta learn that if you don't get it by midnight, chances are you ain't gonna get it, and if you do, it ain't worth it.

> — *Casey Stengel, New York Yankees manager*

W e prefer wham, bam, thank-you-ma'am affairs. In fact, if we're spotted taking a girl out to dinner we're accused of "wining and dining," which is bad form.

> — *Jim Bouton, New York Yankees pitcher*

T oday's players don't even womanize as much as yesterday's. They don't have to. The women manize.

> — *Charles Einstein, sportswriter*

T he only time sex has bothered me is when I do it during the competition.

> — *Bruce Jenner, Olympic decathlon champion*

How to use your leisure time is the biggest problem of a ballplayer.
— *Branch Rickey, Brooklyn Dodgers president*

The trouble with bedchecks is you usually disturb your best players.
— *Dick Siebert, minor league coach*

Chuck Tanner used to have a bedcheck just for me every night. No problem—my bed was always there.
— *Jim Rooker, pitcher*

I've been known to party day and night. Heck, in Las Vegas I paid a guy $50 an hour to sleep for me.
— *Doug Sanders, professional golfer*

I made a vow in church when I was a kid that I would not drink until I was eighteen. I've made up for it since.
— *Billy Martin, New York Yankees manager*

Okay, all you guys act horny.
— *Jim Pagliaroni, Seattle Pilots catcher,*
just before returning from a road trip

He who have fastest cart never have to play bad lie.
— *Mickey Mantle, New York Yankees outfielder*

No. He's mighty handy to have along when you go out drinking beer.
— *Wahoo McDaniel, NY Jets football player,*
on whether the team resents Joe Namath's high salary

The American League has more smut magazines in its clubhouses.
— *Bob Uecker, major league catcher, on the*
difference between the National and American League

They didn't mind after they learned they didn't have to study for them.

> — *Mack Brown, Tulane football coach,*
> *answering his team's reaction to drug tests*

Kevin Mitchell found God in spring training. Then every night he tried to find a goddess.

> — *Len Dykstra, NY Mets outfielder,*
> *on one of his teammates*

I guess creative minds are a function of the kind of rum you drink. Like most good ideas, this one came in the conducive setting of a bar.

> — *George Fitch, U.S. Foreign Services officer,*
> *on how a bobsled team from Jamaica*
> *was entered in the Winter Olympics*

Bobby sighs a little more profanely than I do.

> — *Fred Taylor, Ohio State basketball coach,*
> *on why he doesn't get called on technical fouls*
> *as often as Bob Knight*

I know Munson hasn't done anything wrong. I'd bet my house on it.

> — *Joe Schmidt, Detroit Lions football coach,*
> *on the possibility of Bill Munson*
> *being asked to testify on gambling in Detroit*

There is much less drinking now than there was before 1927, because I quit drinking on May 24, 1927.

> — *Rabbit Maranville, Boston Braves infielder*

Running

Running has given me a glimpse of the greatest freedom that a man can ever know, because it results on the simultaneous liberation of both body and mind.

— *Roger Bannister, runner*

My doctor recently told me that jogging could add years to my life. I think he was right. I feel ten years older already.

— *Milton Berle, comedian*

It's unnatural for people to run around city streets unless they are thieves or victims. It makes people nervous to see someone running. I know that when I see someone running on my street, my instincts tell me to let the dog out after him.

— *Mike Royko, syndicated columnist*

Running for money doesn't make you run fast, it makes you run first.

— *Ben Jipcho, runner*

The art of running the mile consists, in essence, of reaching the threshold of unconsciousness at the instant of breasting the tape.

— *Paul O'Neill, writer*

If I die, I want to be sick.

— *Abe Lemons, Oklahoma City University basketball coach, on why he doesn't run*

The first thing you think about is right at the end of the first lap. You come around and there's a guy holding up a card that says 23 laps to go and you feel sick.

— *Greg Fredericks, long distance runner*

The Inner Game

HOPES AND DREAMS

I want to be the fastest woman in the world, in a manner of speaking.

> — *Shirley Muldowney, drag racer*

When I was a little boy, I wanted to be a baseball player and join the circus. With the Yankees I've accomplished both.

> — *Graig Nettles, New York Yankees infielder*

When I was young I wanted to be the best coach in the nation. Later I just wanted to be the oldest.

> — *John Bridgers, football coach*

All I want out of life is that when I walk down the street, people will say, "There goes the greatest hitter who ever lived."

> — *Ted Williams, Boston Red Sox outfielder*

I don't want to be a hero, I don't want to be a star. It just works out that way.

> — *Reggie Jackson, New York Yankees outfielder*

All I ever wanted to be president of, was the American League.

> — *A. Bartlett Giamatti, Yale University president*

I never wanted them to forget Babe Ruth, I just wanted them to remember Aaron.

> — *Hank Aaron, Atlanta Braves outfielder*

When I said my prayers as a kid, I'd tell the Lord I wanted to be a pro hockey player. Unfortunately, I forgot to mention National Hockey League, so I spent sixteen years in the minors.

> — *Don Cherry, Boston Bruins coach*

I never wanted to be a millionaire, I just wanted to live like one.

> — *Walter Hagen, professional golfer,*
> *in* The Walter Hagen Story

I don't want to be a star. Stars get blamed for too much.

> — *Enos Cabell, Houston Astros infielder*

I'm working as hard as I can to get my life and my cash to run out at the same time. If I can just die after lunch Tuesday, everything will be fine.

> — *Doug Sanders, professional golfer*

When I was a boy growing up in Kansas, a friend of mine and I went fishing and as we sat there in the warmth of a summer afternoon on a river bank we talked about what we wanted to do when we grew up. I told him I wanted to be a major league baseball player, a genuine professional like Honus Wagner. My friend said that he'd like to be President of the United States. Neither of us got our wish.

> — *Dwight David Eisenhower, thirty-fourth*
> *President of the United States*

I don't have some long-range goal that I've always wanted to do after I grew up. What am I supposed to say? Yeah, I'm forty-three, and when I'm through with golf I'd like to be an astronaut?

> — *Lee Trevino, professional golfer*

First year, a .500 season. Second year, a conference championship. Third year, undefeated. Fourth, a national championship. And by the fifth year, we'll be on probation, of course.

> — *Bear Bryant, University of Alabama football coach*

I wanted this one, I wanted the last one, and I want the next one.

> — *Warren Spahn, New York Mets pitcher,*
> *the night he won his 300th game,*
> *quoted by Bob Uecker in* Catcher in the Wry

I told my wife three years ago that my goal was to be a coach by the age of 30. My goal, now, is to still be a coach at the age of 30.

> *— Greg Karpe, 28 year old college basketball coach*

It took Moses 40 years to lead the children of Israel out of the wilderness. Our goal is just to tie him; we can't beat him.

> *— John Bridgers, Baylor football coach,*
> *on their 39 years without a conference championship*

He's more likely to die on a 16-foot yacht with a 60-year old mistress.

> *— Betsy Cronkite, on Walter Cronkite's secret wish*
> *to die on a 60-foot yacht with a 16-year old mistress*

I'd like the body of Jim Brown, the moves of Gale Sayers, the strength of Earl Campbell and the acceleration of O.J. Simpson. And just once, I would like to run and feel the wind in my hair.

> *— Rocky Blier, Pittsburgh Steelers, who is balding*

To get as many goals this year as Wayne Gretzky got last week.

> *— Don Maloney, NY Rangers, on his New Year's wish*

MOTIVATION

When I hit a ball, I want someone else to go chase it.

> — *Roger Hornsby, St. Louis Cardinals infielder,*
> *on why he didn't play golf*

The only reason I ever played golf in the first place was so I could afford to hunt and fish.

> — *Sam Snead, professional golfer*

We're not giving away any football players who could hurt us later. I don't mind people thinking I'm stupid, but I don't want to give them any proof.

> — *Bum Phillips, Houston Oilers coach*

PRESSURE
High Anxiety

Any time you play golf for whatever you've got, that's pressure. I'd like to see H.L. Hunt go out there and play for three billion.

> — *Lee Trevino, professional golfer*

You don't know what pressure is until you play for five bucks with only two in your pocket.

> — *Lee Trevino, professional golfer*

There's no pressure here. This is a lot of fun. Pressure is when you have to go to the unemployment office to pick up a check to support four people.

> — *George Brett, Kansas City Royals infielder*

What do you mean, pressure? In New York, I pitched once when we were trying to keep from losing 100 games. That's pressure.

> — *Nino Espinosa, former New York Mets pitcher*

It's natural to feel it. But you hide it. Show it, and you are through.

> — *Joe Garagiola,* Baseball is a Funny Game

In the pressure games, always bet against the Dallas Cowboys, the San Francisco Giants, and Germany.

> — *Anonymous*

Thirty-two pounds per square inch.

> — *Bill Lee, Montreal Expos pitcher,*
> *describing the pressure of a pennant race.*

Some mornings I didn't really warm-up—just hit enough putts to see what frequency my nerves were on.

> — *Phil Rodgers, professional golfer*

Putting is clutch city. Usually my putting touch deserts me under pressure. From five feet in to the hole you're in the throw-up zone.

> — *Dave Hill, professional golfer*

If this was any other tournament than The Masters, I'd have shot sixty-six. But I was choking out there. That green coat plays castanets with your knees.

> — *Chi Chi Rodriguez, professional golfer*

Wait till she learns how to choke.

> — *Billy Jean King, professional tennis player,*
> *on 14-year-old Tracy Austin's victory*
> *over a high-ranked pro in the U.S. Open*

I developed osteoporosis of the personality. My thought processes became brittle.

> — *Mac O'Grady, professional golfer,*
> *on the effects of pressure*

I don't understand these new coaches who don't drink. What do they do when they get beat?

> — *Abe Lemons, Texas University basketball coach*

Sometimes it's frightening when you see a 19-year old kid running down the floor with your paycheck in his mouth.

> — *Bob Zuffelato, Boston College basketball coach,*
> *on pressure*

I hit a hook that went so far out of bounds I almost killed a horse in some stables a cab ride from the first fairway. I was so nervous I didn't have the strength to push the tee in the ground.

> — *Mike Souchak, professional golfer,*
> *on his first professional tournament*

You gotta' sleep before you have nightmares.

> — *Bep Giudolin, Kansas City Scouts coach,*
> *when asked if he had nightmares about his team*

SUPERSTITION

Everytime I fail to smoke a cigarette between innings the opposition will score.

> — *Earl Weaver, Baltimore Orioles manager*

I don't like to jump from tall buildings before big games.
> — *John Campana, Bucknell University lineman*

I have only one superstition: I make sure to touch all the bases when I hit a home run.

> — *Babe Ruth, New York Yankees outfielder*

I have two: One, don't call someone a bad name if they have a loaded pistol. Two, don't call your girlfriend Tina if her name is Vivien.

> — *George Underwood,*
> *East Tennessee State University forward*

Superstitious people don't discuss their superstitions.

> — *Rusty Staub, New York Mets pinch-hitter*

My only feeling about superstition is that it's unlucky to be behind at the end of the game.

> — *Duffy Daugherty, Michigan State football coach*

I don't change girlfriends too often during the season.

> — *Robert Foote, Simpson College basketball star*

I'm superstitious and every night I got a hit, I ate Chinese food and drank tequila. I had to stop hitting or die.

> — *Tim Flannery, San Diego Padres,*
> *when he had a 14 game hitting streak*

I feel like Job. I can't get mad at anybody except the Lord, and if I do that, I'm afraid things will get worse.

— Sandy Koufax, Los Angeles Dodgers pitcher, following an injury

One of my players said he wished they wouldn't play that song. I asked him why. He said every time they played it he had a bad day. The song was the Star Spangled Banner.

— Jim Leyland, Pittsburgh Pirates manager

If it was a foul, I hope the Lord strikes me down right here on the spot . . . See, I told you.

— Babe McCarthy, Memphis Pros basketball coach, on a bad call

SILENT PRAYERS

May this unknown fellow across from me be skinny, slow, weak, stupid and love football but hate body contact.

> — *Ron Mix, San Diego Chargers tackle*

I once said coaching a first-year team was a religious experience. You do a lot of praying, but most of the time the answer is "No."

> — *Bill Fitch, NBA coach*

Some coaches pray for wisdom. I pray for 260 pound tackles. They'll give me plenty of wisdom.

> — *Chuck Mills, Wake Forest football coach*

No, we've got so many things to pray for, we'd be penalized 15 yards for delaying the start of the game.

> — *Fred Casoti, Colorado University assistant athletic director,*
> *if the football team prayed before games*

I called up Dial-a-Prayer, and they hung up on me.

> — *Mack Brown, Tulane football coach*
> *when his team was 0-7.*

I don't think God cares that we're not hitting. If he did, then Billy Graham would be hitting .400.

> — *Chris Sabo, Cincinnati Reds infielder, when owner Marge*
> *Schott asked if prayers would help the team*

Physical and Mental Traits

PHYSIQUE

The best use of fat since the invention of bacon.

> — *Ray Sons, Chicago Sun Times columnist,*
> *on William "The Refrigerator" Perry*

We don't have any refrigerators. We have a few pot-belly stoves, but they're on the coaching staff.

> — *Dave Curry, University of Cincinnati football coach*

As a kid, I was big for my age. Now I'm big for anybody's age.

> — *Joe Barry Carroll, Golden State Warriors center*

Frank Howard is so big, he wasn't born, he was founded.

> — *Jim Murray, sportswriter*

I'm wall-to-wall and treetop tall.

> — *Dave Parker, Pittsburgh Pirates outfielder*

You should have seen how little I was when I was a kid. I was so small that I got my start in golf as a ball marker.

> — *Chi Chi Rodriguez, professional golfer*

Watching Fernando Valenzuela force himself into a Los Angeles Dodgers uniform is something like seeing Kate Smith struggling to fit into a pair of Brooke Shields' designer jeans.

> — *H.G. Reza, sportswriter*

I don't take anything to alter the physiological condition of my body—it's running too perfectly on eighty-two percent body fat.

> — *Doug Rader, Texas Rangers manager*

Everything worthwhile in life is worth a price. Some people give their bodies to science, I give mine to baseball.

> — *Ron Hunt, Montreal Expos infielder,*
> *on setting the record for being hit by a pitch*

A catcher and his body are like the outlaw and his horse. He's got to ride that nag till it drops.

> — *Johnny Bench, Cincinnati Reds catcher*

Doctors tell me I have the body of a 30-year-old. I know I have the brain of a 15-year-old. If you've got both, you can play baseball.

> — *Pete Rose, Cincinnati Reds player-manager*

I'm as tall as I can be.

> — *Alvin Adams, Phoenix Suns, who is 6' 9",*
> *if he felt he was too small to play center*

I have a furniture problem. My chest has fallen into my drawers.

> — *Billy Casper, professional golfer*

If Boog Powell held out his right hand, he'd be a railroad crossing.

> — *Joe Garagiola, former Pittsburgh Pirates catcher*

George McGinnis's hands are so huge I'll bet he's able to Palm Sunday.

> — *Peter Vecsy, sportswriter*

Joe has a 22-year-old body and 70-year-old knees.

> — *Anonymous teammate, on Joe Namath,*
> *New York Jets quarterback*

They examined all my organs. Some of them are quite remarkable, and others are not so good. A lot of museums are bidding on them.

> — *Casey Stengel, New York Mets manager,*
> *after a checkup*

I was 6' 1" when I started boxing, but with all the uppercuts I'm up to 6' 5".
— *Chuck Wepner, heavyweight contender*

When I tee the ball where I can see it, I can't hit it. And when I put it where I can hit it, I can't see it.
— *Jackie Gleason, comedian, on his wide middle*

For his salad, you just pour vinegar and oil on your lawn and let him graze.
— *Jim Bakken, St. Louis Cardinals,
on 280 pound teammate Bob Young*

When we stick him in the whirlpool, we gotta have a lifeguard there.
— *Bobby Bowton, Florida State football coach,
on 5'8", 135 pound kicker, Dave Cappelan*

He's built like no one else in the world. His arms start at his ears.
— *Marty Howe, on his father, Gordie Howe*

Sure I was once a 97-pound weakling. When I was four years old.
— *Paul Anderson, 375 pound weightlifter*

You can eat anything you want, as long as you don't swallow it.
— *Archie Moore, ex-lightweight champion,
on how to control your weight*

I'd rather be the shortest player in the majors than the tallest player in the minors.
— *Freddie Patek, 5'5", 148 pound baseball player
for the California Angels*

I don't know, but I stepped on a scale that gives fortunes and the card read "Come back in 15 minutes alone."
— *Frank Layden, Utah Jazz coach, on his weight*

Like putting just one more suitcase on the Queen Mary.

> — *Kent Biggerstaff, Pittsburgh Pirates trainer,*
> *when Rick Reuschel added 4 pounds*
> *to his 240 pound weight*

I went to the doctor and asked how I could improve my sex life. He told me to run 20 miles a day and to take off 40 pounds. I called him 2 weeks later to tell I had been running 20 miles a day and had lost 40 pounds. He asked how my sex life was and I told him I didn't know, I was 280 miles away.

> — *Frank Layden, Utah Jazz coach*

What are you going to eat? Redwoods?

> — *John Candelaria, Pittsburgh Pirates, to big*
> *Dave Parker thinking of being a vegetarian*

Charles joined my family for a day at the beach last summer and my children asked if they could go into the ocean. I had to tell them, "Not right now, Charles is using it."

> — *Pat Williams, Philadelphia 76ers, on Charles Barkley*

With parents 6'7" and siblings 6'7" and 6'3", I never worried if I was adopted.

> — *Chuck Nevitt, 7'5" Detroit Pistons center*

Good thing William "Refrigerator" Perry didn't need acupuncture. They'd have to use a harpoon.

> — *Buddy Baron, Cincinnati radio show host*

If I ever lose my luggage, I know where to go to borrow clothes.

> — *Mike Fratello, Atlanta Hawks coach, on the plus side*
> *of having Spud Webb on his team (they are both 5'7")*

When we go to a restaurant, we don't look at the menu. We get an estimate.

> — *Willie Jeffries, Howard University football coach*

No, but I've never been mistaken for anyone else.

— Rosie Greer, Los Angeles Rams 300-pound tackle,
when he was asked if he had a middle initial

It's tough to be fit as a fiddle when you're shaped like a cello.

— Frank Layden, Utah Jazz basketball coach,

Just because somebody is small doesn't mean he can't play in the NBA. Tyrone Bogues is 5 feet 3 inches. That's tall enough. Four feet, that would be too small.

— Manute Bol, Washington Bullets

The biggest problem Muggsy will have is when he sits on the bench, his feet won't hit the floor.

— Tom Newell, NBA coach, when
he saw 5'3" Tyrone Bogues

You have to be 6'10" and weigh 220 pounds to get away with it.

— Bill Russell, Boston Celtics basketball star,
wearing a fancy-laced shirt

At a party, it's a great ice-breaker.

— Chuck Nevitt, Detroit Pistons basketball player,
on the benefit of being 7'5"

If he didn't have that Adam's apple, there would be no shape to his body at all.

— Lee Trevino, pro golfer, on announcer Chris Schenkel

He was eating things we wouldn't even go swimming with in Alabama.

— Charles Hannah, Tampa Bay Buccaneers lineman,
watching coach Abe Gibon consume a huge amount of
exotic dishes

She probably felt I should have won.

> — *Chip Kell, Tennessee football player, on how his wife felt when he was the runner-up in the Ugliest-Man-on-Campus contest*

I'm 5 feet 15 inches tall.

> — *Carol Mann, pro golfer, on how tall she is*

His manager likes to call him "Bulldog", but if Orel were a canine, he'd probably be wearing a jeweled collar... If he was any paler, he could haunt a house.

> — *Jim Murray, sportswriter, LA Times, on Orel Hershiser*

They are so big they can double-team us with one man.

> — *Rick Forzano, Navy football coach, on Notre Dame*

All the fat guys watch me and say to their wives, "See? That fat guy's doing OK. Bring me another beer."

> — *Mickey Lolich, Detroit Tigers pitcher, who is overweight*

He makes a great hitting background.

> — *Richie Ashburn, Phillies announcer, on John McSherry, 300 pounds, umpiring at second base*

When I saw her coming, I hollered for the police. I thought someone stole the ball bag.

> — *Frank Layden, Utah Jazz manager, describing Morganna, the Kissing Bandit*

SELF-EFFACEMENT

I'm just a caraway seed in the bakery of life.

— *Pete Gillen, on being Xavier University basketball coach*

Why am I a catcher? Look at this equipment. You know what they call this stuff? The tools of ignorance. Does that answer the question?

— *Steve Yeager, Los Angeles Dodgers catcher*

We were the quintessence of athletic atrocity.

— *Mike Newlin, Houston Rockets guard*

We set Monday Night Football back 2,000 years. They beat us in every phase of the game—passing, running, kicking, special teams and coaching. They even beat us coming out of the tunnel.

— *John McKay, coach, Tampa Bay Buccaneers*

We're not real fast. In fact, we had three loose balls roll dead in practice the other day.

— *Les Wothke, Western Michigan University basketball coach*

In our first three games this season we didn't fumble. In our fourth game we fumbled ten times. This shows you what an extra week of coaching will do.

— *Duffy Daugherty, Michigan State University football coach*

People say I'm not a happy man. I am. It's just that sometimes I forget to tell my face.

— *Lavell Edwards, Brigham Young University football coach*

If the meek are going to inherit the earth, our offensive linemen are going to be land barons.

— *Bill Muir, Southern Methodist University football coach*

The fans like to see home runs, and we have assembled a pitching staff for their enjoyment.

— *Clark Griffith, Minnesota Twins executive*

I don't want to knock our offensive power, but to save time the ground crew could drag the infield during batting practice.

— *Merv Rettenmund, Texas Rangers batting coach*

I shot a Red Grange today—seventy-seven. Somebody should have shot me. I looked like I needed a white cane.

— *Tom Watson, professional golfer*

I'm not sure that I've changed all that much. They just found somebody worse.

— *Jimmy Connors, professional tennis player, on his attitude*

I putted like Joe Schmoe. And I'm not even sure Joe would appreciate that.

— *Arnold Palmer, professional golfer*

If Jack Nicklaus had to play my tee shots, he couldn't break eighty. He'd be a pharmacist with a string of drugstores in Ohio.

— *Lee Trevino, professional golfer*

Errors are part of my image.

— *Dick "Dr. Strangeglove" Stuart, Phillies infielder*

I'm the only man in the history of the game who began his career in a slump and stayed in it.

— *Rocky Bridges, former Cincinnati Red*

I'm working on a new pitch. It's called a strike.

— *Jim Kern, Cleveland Indian*

I was the worst hitter ever. I never even broke a bat until last year. Then I was backing out of the garage.

— *Lefty Gomez, former New York Yankees pitcher*

Prorated at five hundred bats a year, that means that for two years out of the fourteen I played, I never even touched the ball.

— *Norm Cash, former Detroit Tiger,*
on his 1,081 career strikeouts

I'm getting by on three pitches now: a curve, a change-up, and whatever you want to call that thing that used to be called my fastball.

— *Frank Tanana, California Angels pitcher*

I'm just a garbage man. I come into a game and clean up other people's mess.

— *Dan Quisenberry, Kansas City Royals relief pitcher*

You couldn't play on my Amazing Mets without having held some kind of record, like one fella held the world's international all-time record for a pitcher getting hit on the ankles.

— *Casey Stengel, New York Mets manager*

I'm not a Mercedes, but a Volkswagen: I don't go fast, but you can get a lot of mileage out of me.

— *Dan Quisenberry, Kansas City Royals pitcher*

Why am I wasting so much dedication on a mediocre career?

— *Ron Swoboda, New York Mets outfielder*

I think the whole game hinged on one call—the one I made last April scheduling the game.

— *Pete Gavett, University of Maine*
women's basketball coach, on a lopsided loss

I went through life as the "player to be named later."

> — *Joe Garagiola, former Pittsburgh Pirates catcher*

The only thing we led baseball in was team meetings.

> — *Richie Zisk, Seattle Mariners outfielder*

I've got a hitch in my swing and I hit off the wrong foot. I've done it the wrong way my whole career.

> — *Hank Aaron, Milwaukee Braves outfielder*

Me carrying a briefcase is like a hog wearing earrings.

> — *Sparky Anderson, Detroit Tigers manager*

I've got one advantage: when you're as slow as I am, you don't lose any speed as you grow older.

> — *Howard Twilley, Miami Dolphins receiver*

Everywhere I go there's interest in Georgia Tech basketball. But then, I only go to places where there's interest in Georgia Tech basketball.

> — *Dwane Morrison, Georgia Tech basketball coach*

Every year we go to a minor bowl. If they have a Soybean Bowl next year, we'll be in it.

> — *Jake Staples, Louisiana State University athletic director*

The day I got a hit off Koufax was when he knew it was all over.

> — *Sparky Anderson, former Philadelphia Phillies infielder*

Sporting goods companies offered to pay me not to endorse their products.

> — *Bob Uecker, Catcher in the Wry*

In twenty years I'll be the answer to the sports trivia question, 'Who played center for UCLA between Lew Alcindor and Bill Walton?'

> — *Steve Patterson, UCLA basketball*

I don't mind hate mail, but when a letter comes to the station addressed, "Jerk, KSFO, San Francisco," and I get it, then I start to worry.

— Lon Simmons, San Francisco Giants announcer

We didn't want to weaken the rest of the league.

— Frank Lane, Milwaukee Brewers executive,
on why he didn't make any off-season trades

I wanted to go into my home run trot, but I realized I didn't have one.

— Jim Essian, Chicago White Sox catcher,
on his first major league homer

Anybody with ability can play in the big leagues. But to be able to trick people year in and year out the way I did, I think that's a much greater feat.

— Bob Uecker, sportscaster and former catcher

I have never considered myself a great talent. I think I have gotten more publicity for doing less than any other player who ever lived.

— Bo Belinsky, Philadelphia Phillies pitcher

I've been good for team unity, because everybody hates the same guy.

— Buddy Ryan, Philadelphia Eagles head coach

They're going to retire my uniform—with me in it.

— Steve Hovley, Oakland A's outfielder

I can airmail the golf ball, but sometimes I don't put the right address on it.

— Jim Dent, professional golfer

My game is impossible to help. Ben Hogan said every time he gave me a lesson it added two shots to his game.

— Phil Harris, comedian

If this was a prize fight, they'd stop it.

— Bob Hope, comedian, on his golf game

No matter how hard I try, I just can't seem to break sixty-four.

— *Jack Nicklaus, professional golfer*

The highlight of my career? Oh, I'd say that it was in 1967 in St. Louis. I walked with the bases loaded to drive in the winning run in an intrasquad game in spring training.

— *Bob Uecker, sportscaster*

Was Wayne Gretsky sick?

— *Larry Robinson, Montreal Canadiens defenseman, on being voted Player of the Week*

I admire the loyalty of Minnesotans. They voted for Mondale, and they keep watching us.

— *Lou Holtz, University of Minnesota football coach*

I don't say my golf game is bad, but if I grew tomatoes they'd come up sliced.

— *Miller Barber, professional golfer*

Oh, no. I've been at it much too long and have too much experience. I'd say I'm a Space Captain.

— *Muffin Spencer-Devlin, professional golfer, denying she's a Space Cadet*

I'm the oratorical equivalent of a blocked punt.

— *Hayden Fry, Southern Methodist University football coach*

I've got a face made for radio.

— *Ron Luciano, former major league umpire, on his short-lived career as a television commentator*

Before the end, it kind of felt like we were the team that the Globetrotters play all the time.

— *Ron Wooten, New England Patriots lineman, on the Pat's one-sided loss to the Chicago Bears in the Super Bowl*

I got tired of ducking line drives and backing-up home plate.

> — *Bob Miller, former New York Mets*
> *pitcher, on why he retired*

I mighta' been able to make it as a pitcher, except for one thing. I had a rather awkward motion and every time I brought my left arm forward I hit myself in the ear.

> — *Casey Stengel, New York Yankees manager*

A lot of long relievers are ashamed to tell their parents what they do. The only nice thing about it is that you get to wear a uniform like everybody else.

> — *Jim Bouton, New York Yankees pitcher*

So I'm ugly. So what? I never saw anyone hit with his face.

> — *Yogi Berra, New York Yankees catcher*

I owe everything to golf. Where else could a guy with an IQ like mine make this much money?

> — *Hubert Green, professional golfer*

I owe my success to expansion pitching, a short right-field fence, and my hollow bats.

> — *Norm Cash, Detroit Tigers outfielder*

It took me seventeen years to get three thousand hits in baseball. I did it in one afternoon on the golf course.

> — *Hank Aaron, Atlanta Braves outfielder*

My best score is 103, but I've only been playing fifteen years.

> — *Alex Karras, former football star, on golf*

I'm an easy guy to dislike.

> — *Charles Barkley, Philadelphia 76ers forward*

BRUTE FORCE

I taught Jack a lot, how to tie his shoes, how to brush his fangs.

> — *Ray Mansfield, Pittsburgh Steelers, on Jack Lambert*

I don't have a name for my favorite hold. I just grab them and keep the pressure on until they stop wiggling.

> — *Ernie Ladd, San Diego Chargers 300-pound*
> *tackle, and part-time wrestler*

Linebacker Dick Butkus and tackle Archie Sutton hit me at the same time. Each grabbed a leg and was pulling away when Butkus said, "O.K., Archie, make a wish."

> — *Craig Morton, California Bears quarterback,*
> *who played against the two in college*

I can be found the next couple of months trying to perfect my new punch— the lipbuttoner.

> — *Archie Moore, heavyweight fighter,*
> *on a proposed match with Cassius Clay*

When he goes on a safari, the lions roll up the windows.

> — *Monte Clark, Detroit Lions football coach,*
> *on the tough Larry Zonka*

We were tipping our plays. Whenever we broke from the huddle, three backs were laughing and one was pale as a ghost.

> — *John Breen, general manager of the*
> *last place Houston Oilers*

It's kind of like comparing the Atlantic and Pacific Oceans. They'll both drown you.

> — *Jim Dickey, Kansas State football coach,*
> *on the 1971 and 1978 Oklahoma teams*

LOOKING GOOD

I love doubleheaders. That way I get to keep my uniform on longer.

> — *Tom Lasorda, Los Angeles Dodgers manager*

There's something about the Yankee uniform that gets you. I think it's the wool—it itches.

> — *Joe Gallagher, New York Yankees outfielder*

You trying to ask me do I wear girdles and bras and the rest of that junk? What do you think I am, a sissy?

> — *Babe Didrikson Zaharias, professional golfer*

They look like a jar of mustard.

> — *Norm Miller, San Diego Padres, on their uniforms*

Uh, oh, I'd better put my teeth in.

> — *Ken Payne, Philadelphia Eagles, on hearing*
> *that a woman sportswriter was in the locker room*

Dressing a pool player in a tuxedo is like putting whipped cream on a hot dog.

> — *Minnesota Fats, pool hustler, on players in a*
> *tournament playing pool in black tie*

John is one man who doesn't let success go to his clothes.

> — *Mike Ditka, Chicago Bears, on John Madden*

This is a sport where you talk about sequins, earrings and plunging necklines—and you are talking about the men.

> — *Christine Brennan, Wash. Post writer, on figure skating*

THE NUMBERS GAME
(Statistics)

A baseball fan has the digestive apparatus of a billy goat. He can, and does, devour any set of diamond statistics with insatiable appetite and then nuzzle hungrily for more.

— *Arthur Daley, sportswriter*

Baseball fans love numbers. They like to swirl them around their mouths like Bordeaux wine.

— *Pat Conroy, sportswriter*

Baseball fans are junkies, and their heroin is the statistic.

— *Robert S. Wieder, sportswriter*

Statistics always remind me of the guy who drowned in the river whose average depth was only three feet.

— *Woody Hayes, Ohio State University football coach*

Say you were standing with one foot in the oven and one foot in an ice bucket. According to the percentage people, you should be perfectly comfortable.

— *Bobby Bragan, Milwaukee Braves manager*

Statistics are about as interesting as first base coaches.

— *Jim Bouton, former New York Yankees pitcher*

Statistics are like a bathing suit, revealing everything except what is important.

— *John Mosedale,* The Greatest of All

They both show a lot, but not everything.

— *Toby Harrah, Cleveland Indians infielder,*
comparing statistics to a bikini

The only important thing about "time of possession" is who gets to keep the ball after the game is over.

> — *Lou Holtz, University of Notre Dame football coach*

Statistics can be used to support anything, including statisticians.

> — *Bill Lyon, Philadelphia Inquirer reporter*

In some three years I played we won six, lost 17 and tied two. Some statistician with a great capacity for charity has calculated that we won 75% of the games we didn't lose.

> — *Roger M. Blough, former Susquehanna University football player and current chairman of U.S. Steel*

It was all right for him to break all my old records, but I thought he would do it gradually...not all in one afternoon.

> — *Steve Spurrier, former Florida State quarterback, on John Reeves*

Repertoire

My three pitches: my change, my change off my change, and my change off my change off my change.

— *Preacher Roe, Pittsburgh Pirates pitcher*

I have four basic pitches: fastball, curve, slider and change-up, plus eight illegal ones.

— *Tommy John, New York Yankees pitcher*

I was what might be called a straight-ball pitcher in the minor leagues, although there were some people who referred to it as a bounce ball. I had good control, meaning I could pretty much determine into which section of the outfield seats the batter was going to hit the ball. The day one of my coaches asked me how I felt about law enforcement as a career I knew I had to come up with another pitch.

— *Charlie Hough, Los Angeles Dodgers pitcher,*
on how he came to throw the knuckleball

My best pitch is anything the batter grounds, lines or pops in the direction of Rizzuto.

— *Vic Raschi, New York Yankees pitcher,*
on teammate Phil Rizzuto

My three best punches were the chokehold, the rabbit punch and the head butt.

— *Chuck Wepner, former heavyweight boxer*

You have the option of catching it by either end.

— *Johnny Unitas, on Billy Kilmer's wobbly option passes*

REWARDS?

Last year we got official Holiday Bowl watches. This year, the bowl has offered to fix the official Holiday Bowl watches.

> — *Glen Kozlowski, Brigham Young,*
> *playing in the Holiday Bowl*

It's great being a celebrity again. I go home and my wife doesn't make me take out the garbage. I don't even have to pick up my clothes.

> — *George Foreman, after winning seven fights*

I need this like I need another knee operation.

> — *Dick Anderson, on being named president*
> *of the NFL Players Association*

Haven't they suffered enough?

> — *A rabid fan, after Bowie Kuhn gave the former*
> *Iranian hostages lifetime baseball passes*

I NTENSE DEDICATION

I'm not paying much attention to the calendar. Last week, I had to keep telling myself it was Christmas. By the way, is Reagan still president?

> — *Raymond Berry, New England Patriots football coach*

Even though he lived on the beach in college, he didn't have a tan. Now that's a serious player.

> — *Bill Fitch, Houston Rockets basketball coach,*
> *regarding UC Santa Barbara rookie Conner Henry*

Billy Jackson, your wife had a baby at Harris Hospital. She would like to hear from you.

> — *A note on the bulletin board at the Fort*
> *Worth Yacht Club, during a regatta*

I would like to change the statement that I think basketball is a matter of life and death. I feel it's much more important than that.

> — *Lee Rose, North Carolina basketball coach*

GOLF

Golf and sex are about the only things you can enjoy without being good at either one.

— *Jimmy Demaret, professional golfer*

Give me golf clubs, the fresh air and a beautiful partner and you can keep the golf clubs and the fresh air.

— *Jack Benny, comedian*

Golf is played by twenty million mature American men whose wives think they were out having fun.

— *Jim Bishop, writer*

Golf is a good walk spoiled.

— *Mark Twain, writer*

Golf is nobody's game.

— *Willie Mays, former major league outfielder*

If I had my way, any man guilty of golf would be ineligible for any office of trust in the United States.

— *H.L. Mencken, writer*

Golf is an awkward set of bodily contortions designed to produce a graceful result.

— *Tommy Armour, professional golfer*

What golf needs is a fist-fight between Jack Nicklaus and Arnold Palmer on the eighteenth green of a nationally televised tournament.

— *Jean Shepherd, writer*

When the Going Gets Tough

Slumps

Not many people talk to you when you're hitting .195.

> — *Dwight Evans, Boston Red Sox outfielder*

Scallions are the greatest cure for a batting slump ever invented.

> — *Babe Ruth, New York Yankees outfielder*

I was going so bad last week I skipped dinner two days because I was down to 198 and I didn't want anyone saying that I wasn't hitting my weight.

> — *Jesse Barfield, Toronto Blue Jays*

I'm 0-for-August.

> — *Lee May, Baltimore Orioles outfielder*

With the kind of year I had, I'm ready to try anything.

> — *Paul Householder, Cincinnati Reds, after a terrible year, and then announcing his engagement*

A couple of weeks ago I went fishing and on the first cast I missed the lake.

> — *Ben Crenshaw, pro golfer, in a slump*

EXCUSES

Blaming shoes for our loss is like blaming the Johnstown flood on a leaky faucet in Altoona.

> *— Duffy Daugherty, Michigan State football coach, on a comment that the shoes used on the artificial turf were responsible for their loss*

How can a guy win a game if you don't give him any runs?

> *— Bo Belinsky, LA Angels pitcher, excusing his poor pitching and 15-0 loss*

If we hadn't given them those first four touchdowns, it might have been different.

> *— H.K. Reeves, Hokes Bluff high school football coach, after losing 53-0*

It was cold in Connecticut and raining in Maui.

> *— George Foster, NY Mets outfielder, on why he reported to spring training on time*

I'll just plead heredity.

> *— Wade Phillips, coach, and son of Bum Phillips, on what he would say if things didn't go right*

I knew those guys were out there. I just didn't know where.

> *— Buck Williams, NY Nets, on why he did so poorly with assists*

You must try to teach your players that if there are creeps hanging around, there's a reason. It's like when you bring flowers to your wife and say there's no reason. There's a reason.

> *— Al McGuire, commenting on players who associate with gamblers*

SAVING FACE

I think they drafted in alphabetical order.

> *— Brent Ziegler, the last pick in the NFL draft*

What do you expect? I'm not Magic Johnson.

> *— Manute Bol, Washington Bulls 7'6" center, on his first assist, after not having had one for 692 minutes*

I was just in the right place at the right time.

> *— Cesar Geronimo, baseball player, on how he felt when he was the 3,000th strikeout, for both Nolan Ryan and Bob Gibson*

It has been my experience that the fastest man on the football field is the quarterback who has just been intercepted.

> *— Barry Switzer, Oklahoma football coach*

I'll take you and a player to be named later.

> *— Dick Radatz, 6'6" pitcher for the Montreal Expos, choosing to fight Freddie Patek (5'5")*

When a pro quarterback goes back to pass and can't find anyone, he runs for his life. I have a wonderful wife and three children and I want to live.

> *— Otto Graham, former Cleveland Browns quarterback, on the number of yards he gained*

DIRTY TRICKS

I never set out to hurt anybody, unless it was really important, like a league game or something.

> — *Dick Butkus, former Chicago Bears linebacker*

When I was a little boy, my mother told me never to put my fingers in my mouth.

> — *Whitey Ford, NY Yankees star pitcher,*
> *denying his use of the spitball*

I cheated. I always cheat.

> — *Len Dykstra, NY Mets outfielder,*
> *on how he won a 30 yard dash*

We hit the dry side of the ball.

> — *Gene Oliver, Milwaukee Braves infielder,*
> *on hits that won a game against Don Drysdale*

I think maybe I should be meaner, not dirtier. There's a difference. Mean is somewhere between rough and dirty.

> — *George Konik, Los Angeles Blades hockey player*

I am the enforcer. That's why I was out on the streets—to make sure no one else was.

> — *John Matuzak, Los Angeles Raiders, after being fined,*
> *for being out at 3 A.M. on Bourbon Street,*
> *before the Super Bowl game*

If Thomson knew what was coming, he'd never have been in the batter's box. I signalled for a knockdown pitch.

> — *Rube Walker, Brooklyn Dodgers catcher,*
> *on the home run that Bobby Thomson hit in 1951*

SNEAKY DIVERSIONS

I wanted them to get over-confident so we could beat them.

— *Cookie Lavegetto, manager of last place Washington
Senators, stating the NY Yankees would win by 15 games*

OK, we'll start with the irons, then we'll work into the woods.

— *Chi Chi Rodriquez, golf pro,
offering a young lady lessons*

I'd get close to him and breathe on his goggles.

— *John Kerr, retired NBA player,
on the way he would play Kareem Abdul-Jabbar*

PLAYING IT SAFE
(Now it Can be Told Dept.)

Now that I'm retired, I want to say that all defensive linemen are sissies.

> — *Dan Fouts, retired San Diego Chargers quarterback*

After the kind of year we had, I've got to touch all the bases.

> — *Bud Selig, cellar-dwelling Milwaukee Brewers owner, on a vacation abroad, hoping to meet the Pope, and the Chief Rabbi in Jerusalem*

Looking for an empty seat in the second row of Section 5.

> — *Keith Erickson, San Francisco Warriors, when asked what he was doing during a fight on the court*

Man, when you're 2 and 8 you don't mess around with an unsigned fruitcake.

> — *Lee Corso, Indiana football coach, on not having eaten a fruitcake sent to him*

Think what would have happened if I dropped it on my toe.

> — *Bill McClard, Arkansas kicker, on why he no longer shot-puts*

Why should we pound our own guys into the ground? The Oilers are not on the Oilers' schedule.

> — *Bum Phillips, Houston Oilers coach, on why he discourages intrasquad games*

HORSE RACING

He's everything I'm not. He's young, he's beautiful, he has lots of hair, he's fast, he's durable, he has a large bank account, and his entire sex life is ahead of him.

> — *Si Burick, sportswriter, on Secretariat*

It is the difference of opinion that makes horse races.

> — *Mark Twain, writer*

At least seventy percent of all race horses don't want to win.

> — *Eddie Arcaro, jockey*

The horse weighs one thousand pounds and I weigh ninety-five. I guess I'd better get him to cooperate.

> — *Steve Cauthen, jockey*

No horse can go as fast as the money you put on it.

> — *Earl Wilson, syndicated columnist*

If I knew what horse would win, I wouldn't be riding, I'd be betting.

> — *Don Brumfield, jockey, asked to pick a winner*

Yes, I follow the horses. Trouble is, my horses follow other horses.

> — *Joe Frisco, comedian*

Just so they'll know I'm a girl.

> — *Mary Bacon, blonde jockey, on why she wears gold earrings in a race*

Ups & Downs

ON WINNING

Winning isn't everything, it's the only thing.

> — *Red Sanders, Vanderbilt University football coach*
> *(Also credited to Vince Lombardi)*

Winning isn't everything, but making the effort to win is.

> — *Vince Lombardi, Green Bay Packers coach*

There's no room for sentiment in baseball if you want to win.

> — *Frankie Frisch, St. Louis Cardinals manager*

If you don't play to win, why keep score?

> — *Vernon Law, Pittsburgh Pirates pitcher*

How you play the game is for college boys. When you're playing for money, winning is the only thing that matters.

> — *Leo Durocher, Brooklyn Dodgers manager*

The key to winning baseball games is pitching, fundamentals and three-run homers.

> — *Earl Weaver, Baltimore Orioles manager*

When you win, nothing hurts.

> — *Joe Namath, New York Jets quarterback*

Winning can be defined as the science of being totally prepared.

> — *George Allen, Washington Redskins coach*

No matter how good you are, you're going to lose one-third of your games. No matter how bad you are, you're going to win one-third of your games. It's the other third that makes the difference.

> — *Tom Lasorda, Los Angeles Dodgers manager*

There's a certain scent when you get close to winning. You may go a long time without winning, but you never forget that scent.

— Steve Busby, Kansas City Royals pitcher

Everything looks nicer when you win. The girls are prettier. The cigars taste better. The trees are greener.

— Billy Martin, New York Yankees manager

When you win, you eat better, sleep better and your beer tastes better. And your wife looks like Gina Lollobrigida.

— Johnny Pesky, Boston Red Sox manager

Everybody says a tie is like kissing your sister. I guess it's better than kissing your brother.

— Lou Holtz, University of Arkansas football coach

I don't know whether always winning is good. It breeds envy and distrust in others and overconfidence and a lack of appreciation very often in those who enjoy it.

— John Wooden, UCLA basketball coach

Winning is overemphasized. The only time it is really important is in surgery and war.

— Al McGuire, Marquette University basketball coach

Winning isn't as important as doing well individually. You can't take teamwork up to the front office to negotiate.

— Ken Landreaux, Los Angeles Dodgers outfielder

Losers assemble in little groups to share their misery and to bitch about the coaches and the guys in other little groups. Winners assemble as a team.

— Emlen Tunnell, New York Giants defensive back

A winner never whines.

— Paul Brown, Cleveland Browns coach

I don't think you could say we were lucky to win, but I think we were kind of fortunate not to lose.

> — *Rodney Harding, Oklahoma State,*
> *after a narrow victory over San Diego State*

I guess the defense over reacted. I'm slower than they think and that fools them.

> — *Joe Morrison, long-time NY Giant,*
> *after a winning season*

It was a great game if you didn't care who won. I cared.

> — *Lou Holtz, Notre Dame football coach,*
> *after a tough loss*

It is not how you hold your racket, it's how you hold your mind.

> — *Bobby Jones, U.S. Davis Cup team captain,*
> *on what it takes to win*

In 1981, golfer Tom Sieckmann won the Philippine Open, the Thailand Open and the Singapore Open, leaving him second only to the U.S. Marines for victories in the Pacific.

> — *Gary Nuhn, Dayton Daily News writer*

I was once on a team that won 445 games in a row...the Harlem Globetrotters.

> — *Wilt Chamberlain, Los Angeles Lakers,*
> *on their 33 game win streak*

I was playing so good, it was like the hole kept getting in the way of the ball.

> — *Calvin Peete, on winning his first PGA tournament*

It's the one where the player pitches the ball back to the official after scoring a touchdown.

> — *Bear Bryant, on his favorite play*

THRILLS

The most exquisitely satisfying act in the world of golf is that of throwing a club. The full backswing, the delayed wrist action, the flowing follow-through, followed by that unique whirring sound, reminiscent only of a passing flock of starlings, are without parallel in sport.

> — *Henry Longhurst, golf commentator*

Golf is more fun than walking naked in a strange place, but not much.

> — *Buddy Hackett,* The Truth About Golf and Other Lies

The pleasure derived from hitting the ball dead center on the club is comparable only to one or two other pleasures that come to mind at the moment.

> — *Dinah Shore, entertainer*

Collecting my first Social Security check.

> — *Gene Sarazen, golfer, on his greatest thrill*

When I got home, my wife and three children were lined up at the door. She said, "Didn't we mean anything?" So now that victory has gone from first to fifth. It's my marriage, the birth of my three kids, and then the game.

> — *Al Saunders, San Diego Chargers football coach,*
> *after he said the greatest thrill of his life*
> *was beating the Denver Broncos*

I'm cool on the outside, but inside it's like a thousand kids jumping up and down on Christmas morning.

> — *Chuck Foreman, Minnesota running back,*
> *on his unemotional reaction when scoring a touchdown*

TRADING PLACES
Hired & Fired

I gave Lamar Hunt the best 15 years of my life. Then I gave him my two worst and he fired me.

— *Hank Stram, Kansas City Chiefs ex-coach*

All I said was that the trades were stupid and dumb and they took that and blew it all out of proportion.

— *Ron Davis, Minnesota Twins,*
when the press said he was critical of the club's trades

The Mets are engineering a big trade. They're offering two outfielders, three pitchers and two infielders to the Dodgers in exchange for a life-size photograph of Sandy Koufax.

— *George Jessel, comedian*

He's not fired. He's just not rehired.

— *Mike Shaw, NBA Buffalo Braves, on coach Jack Ramsey*

They all want to give me bad players, and I've got enough of those.

— *Stan Kasten, Atlanta Hawks general manager,*
on why he hasn't made any trades

We sometimes forget our daughter's age, but we know she's got 80,000 miles on her.

— *Frank Quiles, Minnesota Twins manager,*
on 12 moves in 12 years

Every February I take a look at the players the Jets have drafted and if I see no guards among them, then I consider that a real good draft.

— *Dave Herman, long-time NY Jets guard,*
on what he thinks is a good draft

I'm not sure which is more insulting, being offered in a trade or having it turned down.

> — *Claude Osteen, Los Angeles Dodgers pitcher*

Give them time. They'll learn.

> — *Rich Kelly, an average player, getting a standing ovation when he was traded to the Phoenix Suns*

Religiously speaking, it is an advancement from a Cardinal to a Saint.

> — *Conrad Dobler, after being traded from St. Louis to New Orleans*

We're united in a common goal...to keep my job.

> — *Lou Holtz, Arkansas football coach, on why he uses two quarterbacks and had no problems*

I looked around the room and nobody else was there, so he had to be talking to me.

> — *Abe Lemons, basketball coach, being fired by the athletic director at Texas*

They've got transmission problems, but instead of changing the transmission, they change a tire.

> — *Garo Yepremian, after being let go by the Tampa Bay Buccaneers*

José was truly the player to be named later.

> — *Rocky Bridges, San Francisco Giants, on José Gonzalez, who changed his name to Uribe*

I assume he wants a team with a good chef.

> — *Charley Winner, Miami Dolphins, on 285-pound Pete Johnson, who wants to be traded*

He's probably been traded to another banquet.

> — *Ray Perkins, Alabama football coach, when*
> *Ken Stabler did not appear at a banquet*

It's like trading chipmunk meat for caviar.

> — *Emmet Ashford, umpire, after coming from*
> *the minor league to the major league*

In my new contract I'm going to ask the Dodgers to pay me by the mile.

> — *Doug Camilli, Dodgers catcher, on going back*
> *and forth from the minors to the majors*

I wish they'd hurry up and name a general manager so I can demand to be traded.

> — *Jawann Oldham, NY Knicks basketball player*

I don't know, but if he does, I want to be the owner.

> — *Gene Michael, after being fired as manager by Steinbrenner,*
> *if Steinbrenner could ever be a manager*

They can't fire me because my family buys too many tickets.

> — *Lavell Edwards, BYU football coach, and one of 14 kids*

Sometimes the best deals are the ones you don't make.

> — *Bill Veeck, Chicago White Sox owner*

You never ask why you were fired, because if you do, they're liable to tell you.

> — *Jerry Coleman, San Diego Padres announcer*

You know when it really hits home? When your kids say to you, 'Does this mean we don't get any more free tickets?'

> — *Mike Murphy, when fired as coach of the L.A. Kings*

HARD KNOCKS

I ain't here and I ain't going to be here for a while...I guess.

> — *Charles Kerfeld, after being sent to the minors,*
> *left this message on his answering machine*

I'd be the last to know. I'm the guy who bought the diner next door to the park in Boston, just before we moved to Milwaukee.

> — *Warren Spahn, Milwaukee Braves pitcher,*
> *on rumor that the club would move to Atlanta*

The biggest surprise is me.

> — *Art Fowler, NY Yankees pitching coach,*
> *when asked of any surprises in the Yankee camp*
> *(George Steinbrenner had fired him three times)*

It's a very critical situation because I've got only two years left on my contract.

> — *Ray Danforth, Tulane basketball coach, predicting*
> *his team was only three years away from being a top*
> *team*

Way to go Arch." "Way to go Jack." What's he going to say to me? "Way to clap"?

> — *Rich Rinaldi, Baltimore Bullets reserve guard,*
> *on the coach's after-game congratulations*

What it means is that the vote to fire me will never be unanimous.

> — *Mike Fratello, Atlanta Hawks basketball coach,*
> *newly appointed to the Hawks' board of directors*

I had a Cadillac offered to me a couple of times. You know how that works. They give you the Cadillac one year, and the next year they give you the gas to get out of town.

> — *Woody Hayes, Ohio State football coach*

I've seen enough guys who were kicked upstairs and then found out they were working in a one-story building.

> — *John Kerr, Chicago Bulls basketball coach, on why he turned down an offer to work in the front office*

I called the suicide hotline. I told them what was happening. They told me to go ahead, I was doing the right thing.

> — *Tommy Lasorda, Los Angeles Dodgers, on his large number of injured players*

We have a lot of pitchers capable of stopping our winning streak.

> — *Bruce Hurst, Boston Red Sox pitcher*

It's like finding out your mother-in-law has a twin sister.

> — *Dick Lynch, New York Giants announcer, after Green Bay received John Jefferson, to team up with John Lofton*

When the real estate man heard that I was the new Navy coach, he was enthusiastic. He told me the resale value of the house I took will be tremendous.

> — *Rick Forzano, new Navy football coach, when buying his home*

Me.

> — *Duffy Daugherty, Michigan State football coach, on who was the most pleased to be returning for a new season*

I've graduated from clipboard to headset.

> — *Cliff Stoudt, Pittsburgh Steelers, after being moved from the number three quarterback to the number two quarterback.*

ON LOSING

Every time you win, you're reborn. When you lose, you die a little.
— *George Allen, Washington Redskins coach*

Show me a good loser, and I'll show you a loser.
— *Red Auerbach, Boston Celtic coach*

They say losing builds character. I have all the character I need.
— *Ray Malavasi, Los Angeles Rams coach*

Show me a good loser in professional sports and I'll show you an idiot. Show me a good sportsman and I'll show you a player I'm looking to trade.
— *Leo Durocher, Brooklyn Dodgers manager*

Show me someone who gets angry once in a while, and I'll show you a guy with a killer instinct. Show me a guy walking down the fairway smiling and I'll show you a loser.
— *Lee Trevino, professional golfer*

If there's such a thing as a good loser, then the game is crooked.
— *Billy Martin, Oakland A's manager*

There never was a champion who to himself was a good loser. There's a vast difference between a good sport and a good loser.
— *Red Blaik, Army football coach*

Rockne wanted nothing but "bad losers." Good losers get into the habit of losing.
— *George Allen, Washington Redskins coach*

I'd rather be a poor winner than any kind of loser.
> — *George S. Kaufman, playwright*

There is nothing as lonely as a loser's dressing room.
> — *Walter Winchell, syndicated columnist*

No one knows what to say in the loser's room.
> — *Muhammad Ali, boxer*

The man who can accept defeat and take his salary without feeling guilty is a thief.
> — *George Allen, Washington Redskins coach*

Most ball games are lost, not won.
> — *Casey Stengel, New York Yankees manager*

There's only one bright side of losing—the phone doesn't ring as much the following week.
> — *Lou Holtz, Arkansas University football coach*

Before you can win a game, you have to not lose it.
> — *Chuck Knoll, Pittsburgh Steelers coach*

Ya gotta lose 'em sometime. When you do, lose 'em right.
> — *Casey Stengel, New York Mets manager*

Losing is the great American sin.
> — *John R. Tunis, writer*

When you're a winner you're always happy, but if you're happy as a loser you'll always be a loser.
> — *Mark "The Bird" Fidrych, Detroit Tigers pitcher*

Winning is a matter of opinion. But losing is a cold reality.

> — *Peter Gent, writer*

The taste of defeat has a richness of experience all its own.

> — *Bill Bradley, New York Knicks forward*

When I was losing, they called me nuts. When I was winning, they called me eccentric.

> — *Al McGuire, former Marquette*
> *University basketball coach*

One loss is good for the soul. Too many losses are not good for the coach.

> — *Knute Rockne, Notre Dame University football coach*

You can learn little from victory. You can learn everything from defeat.

> — *Christy Mathewson, New York Giants pitcher*

If you can't accept losing, you can't win.

> — *Vince Lombardi, Green Bay Packers coach*

Anyone can have an off decade.

> — *Larry Cole, Dallas Cowboys,*
> *after going 11 years between scoring a touchdown*

Let's face the facts. You can only take so many of these great lessons in humility.

> — *Kyle Bartee, Lubock Christian School athletic*
> *committee, when they let the coach go after*
> *two seasons with a 1-18 record*

Every time we win, Reggie Miller thanks the Lord. Every time we lose, they blame me.

> — *Buddy Ryan, Philadelphia Eagles coach*

W e definitely will improve this year. Last year we lost 10 games, this year we only scheduled nine games.

> — *Ray Jenkins, Montana State football coach*

T ommy Lasorda looks like he's just been told there's no cannelloni in the world.

> — *Phil Stone, San Francisco Giants*
> *announcer, after a Dodger loss*

T he thing I remember is that the crowd sang "Maryland, My Maryland" after each touchdown. By the end of the first quarter I knew all the words.

> — *Jack Rothrock, who played against*
> *Maryland and lost 60-6 in 1945*

T his is the battle of the movable defense versus the stoppable force.

> — *Joe Salem, Minnesota football coach,*
> *losing to Northwestern (1-6).*

H ow to shake hands.

> — *Bettina Bunge, tennis pro, on what she learned from*
> *Martina Navratilova after numerous losses to her*

I f a tie is like kissing your sister, losing is like kissing your grandmother, with her teeth out.

> — *George Brett, Kansas City Royals*

T he only difference between me and Jim McMahon is that he throws his clubs farther when he gets mad.

> — *Michael Jordan, Chicago Bulls, when playing*
> *golf with Jim McMahon of the Chicago Bears*

S ure I would. I'd miss him, too.

> — *Frank Broyles, Arkansas athletic director,*
> *when asked if he would still like football coach*
> *Ken Hatfield if he lost half their games*

Playing LSU is like going home late. You know you'll catch hell, but there's not a thing you can do about it.

> — *Bo Hagan, Rice assistant football coach*

Next year we're going to recruit a gambler.

> — *Gene Stallings, Texas A & M football coach,*
> *on losing six straight coin tosses*

Being a ticket scalper in the Meadowlands.

> — *Mike Gminski, last place NY Nets basketball player,*
> *on what he thought was the toughest job in the world*

We don't have a fight song. We'll have a surrender song.

> — *Glen Wilkes, Stetson University basketball coach,*
> *after looking at his tough schedule*

All the losing entries will become entrees.

> — *Jean Lapuyade, restaurant owner,*
> *on a snail race which was about to begin*

Who's the one guy who thinks we can do it?

> — *Mike Gottfried, Kansas football coach,*
> *that the odds were 100-1 against*
> *his team winning the conference*

I don't think our offense could get a first down against high grass.

> — *Roland Ortmayer, LaVerne College football*
> *coach, after his team was shut out*

I've taken this team as far as I can.

> — *Lynn Wheeler, Iowa State women's basketball coach,*
> *leaving the school after losing 14 straight games*

If finishing second was so great, then we'd only run in dual meets.

> — *Guy Kochel, Arkansas State track coach*

Kansas State hasn't won a Big Eight championship in 40 years. I told them if I don't win a championship in the same length of time, I'll resign.

> — *Jim Dickey, Kansas State football coach*

What we have is a highlight slide.

> — *David Courtney, L.A. Kings,*
> *on the team's highlight films*

We're really pleased. This is the highest the Mariners have ever finished.

> — *Chuck Armstrong, Seattle Mariners,*
> *when the team placed third in a local spelling bee*

The last time-out was to take the sandwich orders.

> — *Ed Murphy, Mississippi basketball coach, on why he*
> *took a time-out, with two minutes to play and down by*
> *20 points*

Last year we couldn't win on the road. This year we can't win at home. I don't know where else to play.

> — *Harry Neale, general manager Vancouver*
> *Canucks, on his losing team*

Aches & Pains
Hurting & Injuries

Fractured, hell! The damn thing's broken.

> — *Dizzy Dean, St. Louis Cardinals pitcher*

When they operated on my arm, I asked them to put in Koufax' fastball. They did, but it turned out to be Mrs. Koufax.

> — *Tommy John, Los Angeles Dodgers pitcher*

You never know with these psychosomatic injuries. You have to take your time with them.

> — *Jim Palmer, Baltimore Orioles pitcher*

My problem's behind me now.

> — *George Brett, Kansas City Royals infielder, after hemorrhoid surgery*

I threw up my arms and one just kept going.

> — *Bill Foster, Clemson University basketball coach on how he dislocated a shoulder*

His home address is Disabled List, U.S.A.

> — *Dick Young, sportswriter, on New York Mets outfielder Dave Kingman*

The next time I see a doctor, it better be for an autopsy.

> — *A.J. Duhe, injury-prone Miami Dolphins linebacker*

He sits home and watches his bones mend.

> — *Mrs. Mel Phillips, wife of San Francisco 49ers defensive back Mel Phillips, on what her husband does during the off-season*

There's no pain when I'm walking, but I'm not a walking back.

> — *Edwin Simmons, University of Texas running*
> *back, after knee surgery*

I don't want any doctor building a swimming pool with my knee.

> — *Steve Howe, Los Angeles Dodgers pitcher,*
> *declining surgery*

Who wants to go with a guy who has two bad knees and a quick release?

> — *Connie Stevens, actress,*
> *on Joe Namath, New York Jets quarterback*

My knees look like I lost a knife fight with a midget.

> — *E.J. Holub, Kansas City Chiefs linebacker*

Ninety-five percent of me is very sad that I'm retiring. But my knees are very, very happy.

> — *Dan Dierdorf, St. Louis Cardinals lineman*

I taped a pad to my left ankle because it hurt and I taped the other ankle as a decoy so they wouldn't know which one is injured.

> — *Glenn Doughty, University of Michigan tailback*

I was glad it was his head and not his knee.

> — *Tom Landry, Dallas Cowboys coach,*
> *on an injury to quarterback Roger Staubach*

John Riggins, like Joe Namath, is an enigma wrapped in a bandage.

> — *Larry Merchant, sportswriter*

Waking up from all my operations.

> — *Tim Foley, Miami Dolphins, on what he*
> *loved the most when he was in the NFL*

I learned a long time ago that minor surgery is when they do the operation on someone else, not you.

> — *Bill Walton, San Diego Clippers,*
> *preparing for foot surgery*

The doctors told me there are two things I can't do, play football or dive into empty swimming pools.

> — *John O'Leary, Montreal Alouettes,*
> *after a neck injury*

My first year I broke five ribs, a wrist and a thumb, hurt my knees and sprained two ankles. You don't get hurt when you know what you're doing.

> — *Bob Lilly, Dallas Cowboys tackle*

Pain don't hurt you.

> — *Sparky Anderson, Detroit Tigers,*
> *to an injured Alan Trammell*

The team picture is an x-ray.

> — *John Cirillo, New York Knicks,*
> *who had injuries all season*

My doctor told me if I see two pucks to take the one on the left.

> — *Charlie Simmer, Boston Bruins,*
> *after an injury to his eye*

No, but 11 other guys did.

> — *Gordie Howe, hockey player,*
> *when asked if he had ever broken his nose*

One player broke his nose. How do you go about getting a nose in condition for football.

> — *Darrell Royal, Texas football coach,*
> *when asked if the high rate of injuries*
> *was the result of his team not being in condition*

I thought about bringing in an acupuncturist from Japan. When I heard how much it cost, I called a dart thrower from Tijuana.

— *Ron Newman, soccer coach, on all his injured players*

It's just like a knee injury...except I had it in the head.

— *Ray Perkins, Baltimore Colts, with a serious injury*

Injuries are part of the game. Without them, I wouldn't have a job.

— *Gene Geielmann, St. Louis Cardinal trainer*

I wouldn't say that Joe has a sore arm, per se, but his arm is kind of sore.

— *Weeb Ewbank, NY Jets football coach,*
on Joe Namath missing practice

What was the name of that guy on the Yankees who got hurt and was replaced by Lou Gehrig.

— *Dan Issel, Denver Nuggets, after being*
injured and replaced by Marvin Webster,
who scored 17 points with 17 rebounds

It means I've taken more aspirins than any other player in history.

— *Bob Boone, California Angels catcher, after*
breaking the record for most games caught

He told me, I don't have any pain. So I don't have any pain. But for someone who doesn't have any pain, I'm in pain.

— *Clyde Vaughn, Pittsburgh basketball player, on talking*
to a psychologist who hypnotizes players with injuries

Everywhere, but the roof of my mouth.

— *John Edwards, Houston Astros catcher,*
on where he hurt after a collision at home plate

IT'S ABOUT TIME

They usually show movies on a flight like that.

> — *Ken Coleman, Boston Red Sox*
> *announcer, on a long home run*

It lasted so long I had to trim my nails twice.

> — *Gene Geiselmann, St. Louis Cardinals trainer,*
> *on an extra inning game*

My colleague did three full loads of laundry during the game and didn't miss a play.

> — *Tony Kornheiser, Washington Post columnist,*
> *writing about a very long football game*

Not only could you read a Russian novel, you could write one.

> — *Tony Kornheiser, Washington Post columnist,*
> *writing about a very long football game*

It's like watching Mario Andretti park cars.

> — *Ralph Kiner, announcer, on how boring*
> *it is to watch the knuckleball pitchers*

Bob Gibson pitched as though he's double-parked.

> — *Vince Scully, announcer on a quickly-pitched game*

If you've only got one day to live, come see the Leafs. It'll seem like forever.

> — *Pat Foley, Chicago Blackhawks TV commentator,*
> *on a slow game against Toronto*

She plays like she rented the court for an hour.

> — *A Wimbledon judge when Steffi Graf sped through*
> *her match with Pam Shriver in less than an hour*

TENNIS

A perfect combination of violent action taking place in an atmosphere of total tranquillity.

> — *Billie Jean King, professional tennis player*

Hit at the girl whenever possible.

> — *Bill Tilden, professional tennis player,*
> *on mixed doubles strategy*

When I was forty, my doctor advised me that a man in his forties shouldn't play tennis. I heeded his advice carefully and could hardly wait until I reached fifty to start again.

> — *Hugo L. Black, U.S. Supreme Court Justice*

All tennis courts are alike.

> — *Brad Dillman, actor, on why he*
> *likes tennis more than golf*

He shouldn't pick on girls just because he hasn't had much luck with guys.

> — *Pam Shriver, tennis pro, on Vitas Gerulaitis, who has*
> *been bad-mouthing women's tennis*

They wanted an arm and a leg.

> — *Martina Navratilova, on why she*
> *won't insure her arm*

The Players

ESTEEMED COLLEAGUES

He'd say hello at the start of spring training and good-bye at the end of the season, and the rest of the time he'd let his bat and glove do all the talking for him.

— Ty Cobb, Detroit Tigers outfielder,
on teammate Charlie Gehringer

To him, a game wasn't a mere athletic contest, it was a knock 'em down, crush 'em, relentless war. He was their enemy, and if they got in his way he ran right over them.

— Moe Berg, Chicago White Sox catcher, on Ty Cobb

His trouble is he takes life too seriously. Cobb is going at it too hard.

— Cy Young, Boston Braves pitcher

That goddamn Dutchman is the only man in the game I can't scare.

— Ty Cobb on Honus Wagner, Pittsburgh Pirates infielder

How that man loved to eat. If he'd ever been sawed in half on any given day, I think three-fourths of Stevens' concessions (Yankee Stadium) would have been found inside him.

— Ty Cobb on Babe Ruth, New York Yankees outfielder

The Babe was a great ballplayer, but Cobb was even greater. Babe could knock your brains out, but Cobb would drive you crazy.

— Tris Speaker, Hall of Famer

I'm Billy's best friend, and even I don't like him.

— Whitey Ford, roasting Billy Martin

Could be that he's a nice guy when you get to know him, but why bother?

— Dizzy Dean, St. Louis Cardinals pitcher,
on Bill Terry, New York Yankees infielder

Is a pig pork?

> — *Dizzy Dean, when asked whether*
> *Satchel Paige could really pitch*

He could throw a lamb chop past a wolf.

> — *Arthur "Bugs" Baer, sportswriter,*
> *on Lefty Grove, Philadelphia Athletics pitcher*

Tommy's curve ball had a better hang-time than Ray Guy's punts.

> — *Rocky Bridges, former Cincinnati Reds infielder, on*
> *Tom Lasorda, Los Angeles Dodgers manager*
> *and former minor league pitcher*

Not only is he lucky, he's never wrong.

> — *Whitey Ford, New York Yankees pitcher,*
> *on teammate Yogi Berra*

Everybody who roomed with Mickey said he took five years off their career.

> — *Whitey Ford, New York Yankees pitcher,*
> *on teammate Mickey Mantle*

I got a big charge out of seeing Ted Williams hit. Once in a while they let me try to field some of them, which sort of dimmed my enthusiasm.

> — *Rocky Bridges, Cincinnati Reds infielder*

Bob Gibson is the luckiest pitcher I ever saw. He always pitches when the other team doesn't score any runs.

> — *Tim McCarver, St. Louis Cardinals catcher*

He was something like 0 for 21 the first time I saw him. His first major league hit was a home run off me and I'll never forgive myself. We might have gotten rid of Willie forever if I'd only struck him out.

> — *Warren Spahn, Milwaukee*
> *Braves pitcher, on Willie Mays*

I'm not sure what the hell charisma is, but I get the feeling it's Willie Mays.

> — *Ted Kluszewski, Cincinnati Reds infielder*

Either he throws the fastest ball I've ever seen, or I'm going blind.

> — *Richie Ashburn, Philadelphia Phillies outfielder,*
> *on Los Angeles Dodgers pitcher Sandy Koufax*

The trick against Drysdale is to hit him before he hits you.

> — *Orlando Cepeda, San Francisco Giants infielder,*
> *on Los Angeles Dodgers pitcher Don Drysdale*

I hated to bat against Drysdale. After he hit you, he'd come around, look at the bruise on your arm and say, "Do you want me to sign it?"

> — *Mickey Mantle, New York Yankees outfielder*

Henry Aaron is the only ballplayer I have ever seen who goes to sleep at the plate. But trying to sneak a fastball past him is like trying to sneak the sunrise past a rooster.

> — *Curt Simmons, Philadelphia Phillies pitcher*

Greaseball, greaseball, greaseball. That's all I throw him, and he still hits them. He's the only player in baseball who consistently hits my grease. He sees the ball so well, I guess he can pick out the dry side.

> — *Gaylord Perry, Cleveland Indians*
> *pitcher, on Rod Carew*

He has the uncanny ability to move the ball around as if the bat were some kind of magic wand.

> — *Ken Holtzman, Chicago Cubs pitcher, on Rod Carew*

He can make the ball look so small that you're not even sure there's a practical purpose for being up there.

> — *John Lowenstein, Baltimore Orioles outfielder,*
> *on New York Yankees pitcher Goose Gossage*

Look at Gossage. He's six foot four and most of it is fat. He pitches maybe an inning a week. And for that they pay him a million dollars a year. And you know what? He's worth it.

— Rudy May, New York Yankees pitcher,
on teammate Goose Gossage

If you stand next to Perry, he smells like a drugstore.

— Billy Martin, New York Yankees manager

Blind people come to the park just to listen to him pitch.

— Reggie Jackson, Oakland A's outfielder,
on Tom Seaver, New York Mets pitcher

The only way to pitch him is inside, so you force him to pull the ball. That way, the line drive won't hit you.

— Rudy May, New York Yankees pitcher,
on George Brett, Kansas City Royals infielder

Anybody who has plastic hair is bound to have problems.

— Jay Johnstone, Los Angeles Dodgers outfielder,
on teammate Steve Garvey

How can anyone who runs as slow as you pull a muscle?

— Pete Rose, Cincinnati Reds infielder,
to teammate Tony Perez

Rose wishes he was a wide receiver so he could spike the ball.

— Clint Hurdle, Kansas City Royals outfielder

Pete Rose is the most likable arrogant person I've ever met.

— Mike Schmidt, Philadelphia Phillies infielder

If anybody plays harder than Pete Rose, he's gotta be an outpatient.

> — *Tug McGraw, Philadelphia Phillies relief pitcher*

Tug McGraw has about forty-eight cards in his deck.

> — *Tom Seaver, New York Mets pitcher*

You have to get your uniform dirty. I used to use three uniforms every day. George uses three a month.

> — *Pete Rose, Cincinnati Reds infielder,*
> *on teammate George Foster*

There isn't enough mustard in the world to cover Reggie Jackson.

> — *Darold Knowles, Oakland A's pitcher*

Reggie would give you the shirt off his back. Of course, he'd call a press conference to announce it.

> — *Catfish Hunter, New York Yankees pitcher*

The thing about Reggie is that you know he is going to produce. And if he doesn't, he's going to talk enough to make people think he's going to produce.

> — *Catfish Hunter, New York Yankees pitcher*

When you unwrap a Reggie bar, it tells you how good it is.

> — *Catfish Hunter, New York Yankees pitcher*

I go back to 1965 with Reggie, but I guess I don't go back far enough to remember when he was shy.

> — *Rick Monday, Los Angeles Dodgers outfielder*

When Steve and I die, we are going to be buried in the same cemetery, sixty feet, six inches apart.

> — *Tim McCarver, Philadelphia Phillies catcher,*
> *on his battery-mate, Steve Carlton*

He's baseball's exorcist—scares the devil out of you.

> — *Dick Sharon, Detroit Tigers outfielder,*
> *on Nolan Ryan, California Angels pitcher*

Munson's not moody, he's just mean. When you're moody, you're nice sometimes.

> — *Sparky Lyle, New York Yankees pitcher,*
> *on teammate Thurman Munson*

Wayne Gretsky is going to win two scoring titles this year—the NHL's and the NBA's.

> — *Steve Shutt, Montreal Canadiens wing*

Butkus was unbelievable. I love to see—and listen—to him play. On the sound track of the Bears films, Butkus—when he's going after somebody—sounds like a lion chewing on a big hunk of meat.

> — *Doug Plank, Chicago Bears defensive back,*
> *on teammate Dick Butkus*

He's still the fastest, strongest and most talented center in the league. I say that, hoping that he'll read this and won't hurt me.

> — *Bob Golic, Cleveland Browns defensive lineman,*
> *on Pittsburgh Steelers center Mike Webster*

I wouldn't bet anyone against Byron Nelson. The only time Nelson left the fairway was to pee in the bushes.

> — *Jackie Burke, professional golfer*

When Jack Nicklaus plays well, he wins. When he plays badly, he finishes second. When he plays terrible, he finishes third.

> — *Johnny Miller, professional golfer*

Jack Nicklaus has become a legend in his spare time.

> — *Chi Chi Rodriguez, professional golfer*

Jack Nicklaus is a young Toots Shor—a victim of circumference.

> — *Jimmy Demaret, professional golfer*

They say Sam Snead is a natural golfer. But if he didn't practice, he'd be a natural bad golfer.

> — *Gary Player, professional golfer*

Klem hated my guts and I hated his.

> — *Beans Reardon, major league umpire,*
> *on receiving the 1970 Bill Klem Award*

He's a guy who'll go into a revolving door in the section behind you and come out in front of you.

> — *Paul Richards, Baltimore Orioles manager,*
> *on Branch Rickey, Brooklyn Dodgers general manager*

If I ever run out of ideas for promotions, Charley Finley is finished.

> — *Bill Veeck, Chicago White Sox owner,*
> *on Finley's "borrowing" his ideas*

Lou Holtz can talk faster than I can listen.

> — *Fred Akers, University of Texas football coach*

He has the ability of taking a bad situation and making it immediately worse.

> — *Branch Rickey, Brooklyn Dodgers president,*
> *on his manager, Leo Durocher*

He changed his name from Cohen to Cosell, put on a toupee and "tells it like it is."

> — *Jimmy Cannon, sportswriter*

I tell it like it is. Howard Cosell tells it like Roone Arledge wants it told.

> — *Harry Caray, sportscaster*

I like Howard, I really do. I mean, he's very weird, but I respect him.

> — *Don Meredith, former Dallas Cowboys*
> *quarterback turned sportscaster*

Reggie Jackson wouldn't get into the batter's box until he knew we were back from a commercial. Of course, Uecker wanted to hit during the commercial.

> — *Al Michaels, sportscaster, on colleague Bob Uecker*

It's kind of hard to introduce a guy who you hope gets the flu every Sunday.

> — *Gary Hogeboom, Dallas Cowboy back-up quarterback*

That guy has liquid oxygen in his veins. That's the coldest substance known to man. It's colder than ice water.

> — *Mychal Thompson, on Magic Johnson*

Earl may not be in a class by himself, but whatever class he's in, it doesn't take long to call role.

> — *Bum Phillips, Houston Oilers coach, on Earl Campbell*

He's such a nice guy. But if they had a Naive Bowl, he would coach both sides.

> — *Orville Henry, Arkansas Gazette,*
> *on T.C.U. football coach Jim Shofner*

George is getting to be such a monster that I'd hate to die in a car wreck with the guy. You'd be listed as: Others Killed.

> — *Clint Hurdle, Kansas City Royals outfielder,*
> *on teammate George Brett*

Pete Rose a Hall of Famer? Yes. The Hall of Fame is for baseball. Heaven is for good guys.

> — *Jim Dyer, Montreal Expos*

WHAT'S IN A NAME?

My name used to be O'Connor, but I changed it for business reasons.
> — *Chi Chi Rodriguez, pro golfer*

Yeah, they're Blackie, Toothless, Scarface, and those were just the cheerleaders.
> — *Frank Layden, Utah Jazz coach,*
> *on nicknames when he attended a Brooklyn high school*

Just say it the way it is spelled.
> — *Meriyam Tsalkalamanidze, Russian wrestler,*
> *on how to pronounce his name*

I couldn't pronounce myself.
> — *Bob Miller, NY Mets pitcher,*
> *in changing his name from Gmeinweiser*

To pronounce my name, you take the "par" as in golf, "seg" as in Seagrams whiskey, and "yen" as in Japanese money. Just think of a drunken Japanese golfer.
> — *Ara Parseghian, Notre Dame football coach*

You make a big J, a couple squiggles and some bumps. Who knows the difference?
> — *Marty Januszkiewicz, Baltimore Colts football player,*
> *on how he signs autographs*

I get mail to all kinds of names. Bananas Cavaras, you name it. I didn't mind that, but when one sportswriter called and asked me to spell my first name, that was enough.
> — *Gus Ganakas, Michigan State basketball coach*

Lucky they didn't use my real name. Can you imagine rooting for a horse called Sheldon Greenfield?

> — *Shecky Greene, comedian, on a horse named after him*

I would change it, but momma and daddy must have had something in mind when they gave me the name.

> — *U.L. Washington, Kansas City Royals, on his name U.L.*

Our nickname is the Crusaders, and if this isn't one, then I don't know what is.

> — *Barry Davis, University of Dallas basketball team*
> *coach, after his team had lost 75 straight games*

I dropped the Greek spelling long ago. I could never remember how to spell it myself.

> — *Dee Andrus, Oregon State football coach, on his name*
> *change from Demosthenes Konstandies Andrecopolous*

My mother called me Cupcake, my father called me Doughnut, and the family settled on Cookie.

> — *Cookie Gilchrist, Buffalo Bills running back,*
> *explaining how he got his name*

He was always getting burned.

> — *Bill Parcells, NY Giants football coach,*
> *on how cornerback Elvis Patterson got the name Toast*

Everybody thinks my name is Jerry Laitis, and they call me Mr. Laitis. What can you do when you have a name that sounds like a disease.

> — *Vitas Gerulaitis, tennis star, on his name*

He's doing a great job. If anybody could spell his name, he'd be coach of the year.

> — *Abe Lemons, Texas basketball coach,*
> *on Army coach Mike Krzyzewski*

HEADLINERS

He sat right where I usually sit. I didn't have the heart to say, "move over."

> — *Joe Altobelli, Baltimore Orioles manager,*
> *when President Reagan sat in the dugout*

Oh yeah? Well, I had a better year than he did.

> — *Babe Ruth, New York Yankees outfielder, told*
> *his $80,000 salary was more than the president's*

Yeah? What league was he in?

> — *Pete Browning, Cincinnati Redlegs outfielder,*
> *on hearing of the death of President James Garfield*

King Gustav of Norway: Sir, you are the greatest athlete in the world.

Jim Thorpe: Thanks, King.

Hot as hell, ain't it Prez?

> — *Babe Ruth, New York Yankees outfielder,*
> *to President Calvin Coolidge*

How do you do, Mr. Prime Minister. Ever shake hands with a Mexican before?

> — *Lee Trevino, to British Prime Minister Edward*
> *Heath*

Nice to meet ya, King.

> — *Casey Stengel, Boston Braves outfielder,*
> *to George V of England*

Put your ass into the ball, Mr. President.

> *— Sam Snead, professional golfer,*
> *to President Dwight D. Eisenhower*

Come on Sandy, baby, loosen up. You're too tight.

> *— John Riggins, Washington Redskins running back, to*
> *U.S. Supreme Court Justice Sandra Day O'Connor at a*
> *Washington dinner, just before he passed out*

Excuse me. Somebody important just came in.

> *— Toots Shor, restaurateur, to Sir Alexander*
> *Fleming, inventor of penicillin, on seeing*
> *Mel Ott enter the room*

Were you in the war?

> *— Babe Ruth, New York Yankees outfielder,*
> *to Marshal Foch, World War I hero*

The trouble with Gerry Ford is he played too many games without a helmet.

> *— Lyndon Baines Johnson, thirty-sixth President of the*
> *United States, on Gerald R. Ford, thirty-eighth President*
> *of the United States*

I asked him for a pardon.

> *— John Tonell, New York Islanders,*
> *who had been arrested for drunk driving,*
> *on what he said when he met President Reagan*

I take a national view of the American League and an American view of the National League.

> *— Hubert Humphrey, on his favorite*
> *to win the World Series*

We're looking forward to a great season at the University of California, if we find a way to put cleats on their sandals.

> *— Ronald Reagan, California Governor*

M e and L.B.J., the two strongest Democrats in the country.

> *— Norbert Schemansky, weightlifting champion*
> *and candidate for office in Michigan*

Y es. A lot more golfers beat me.

> *— Dwight Eisenhower, when asked if he noticed*
> *a difference in his golf game, after he no longer*
> *was President*

I was in a lot of sports in high school. But when I saw the size of some of the people on the football team, I went out for the debating team. I've been open-mouthed ever since.

> *— Walter Mondale, University of Minnesota*

P resident Ford waits until he hits his first drive to know what course he's playing that day.

> *— Bob Hope, comedian*

T he last time I played a round with Vice President Agnew he hit a birdie, an eagle, a Moose, an Elk and a Mason.

> *— Bob Hope, comedian*

B aseball without fans is like Jayne Mansfield without a sweater. That can be taken two ways.

> *— Richard Nixon*

H ey Ernie, how ya' doin'? What paper you write for?

> *— Yogi Berra, on being introduced to Ernest Hemingway*
> *and being told he was a famous writer*

CITY & PARK BASHING

On the Road

The girls [in Los Angeles] all look like Brigitte Bardot. Come to think of it, some of the men do, too.

> — *Jim Murray,* The Best of Jim Murray

What scares the hell out of me is waking up dead some morning in the Hyatt Hotel in Oakland.

> — *Earl Weaver, Baltimore Orioles manager*

Fayetteville isn't the end of the world, but you can see it from there.

> — *Lou Holtz, football coach*

The only trouble with Spokane, Washington as a city, is that there's nothing to do there after 10 o'clock—in the morning.

> — *Jim Murray, sportswriter*

When someone in Green Bay says he has a good wardrobe, it means he has ten bowling shirts.

> — *Greg Koch, Miami Dolphins defensive lineman*

In Cincinnati after two o'clock, the only people you see are bartenders, ballplayers and cab drivers.

> — *Jim Brosnan, pitcher*

I went through Cleveland one day and it was closed.

> — *Jay Johnstone, New York Yankees outfielder*

The only good thing about playing in Cleveland is that you don't have to make road trips there.

> — *Richie Scheinblum, Cleveland Indians outfielder*

The only difference between Cleveland and the Titanic is that the Titanic had better restaurants.

> — *Barney Nagler, sportswriter*

In Cleveland, pennant fever usually ends up being just a forty-eight hour virus.

> — *Frank Robinson, former Cleveland Indians manager*

Houston is the only town where women wear insect repellent instead of perfume.

> — *Richie Ashburn, Philadelphia Phillies outfielder*

Oklahoma City is nice if you bring enough Alka-Seltzer.

> — *Bo Belinsky, Philadelphia Phillie pitcher*

Kansas City wasn't the fun spot in my day that it is now.

> — *Casey Stengel, New York Yankees manager*

It's a little like living in purgatory: It's not exactly heaven, but it isn't hell.

> — *Don Klosterman, Kansas City Chiefs scout, on Kansas City*

Boston has two seasons: August and winter.

> — *Billy Herman, Boston Red Sox manager*

The only trouble with Baltimore is it's in Baltimore.

> — *Reggie Jackson, California Angels outfielder*

Pittsburgh is such a tough town even the canaries sing bass there.

> — *Arthur "Bugs" Baer, sportswriter*

I'd want this town on my side if we had to go to war again.

> — *Terry Bradshaw, Pittsburgh Steelers quarterback, on Pittsburgh*

Philadelphia: where they never recognize a trend until it's a tradition.

— *Barney Nagler, sportswriter*

I come from New York, where if you fall down, someone will pick you up by your wallet.

— *Al McGuire, Marquette basketball coach*

I could never play in New York. The first time I came into a game there, I got in the bullpen car and they told me to lock the doors.

— *Mike Flanagan, Baltimore Orioles pitcher*

The good news is that we may stay in San Diego. The bad news, I guess, is the same thing.

— *Buzzy Bavasi, San Diego Padres president*

Dallas is a squeaky-clean city. Roger Staubach is Mr. Straight. Nice, clean, bright uniforms and stadium. Pittsburgh? They call it a shot-and-beer town. Hard-working guys with stumpy legs. A team with mean-looking black uniforms. Nothing squeaky-clean about Pittsburgh.

— *Rocky Bleir, Pittsburgh Steelers running back*

Philadelphia is the only city in the world where you can experience the thrill of victory and the agony of reading about it the next day.

— *Mike Schmidt, Philadelphia Phillies infielder*

At the ball games, the fans stand up for the National Anthem, and by the sixth inning they're just sitting back down.

— *Bob Uecker, sportscaster, on Sun City, Arizona*

I hit 2 balls and killed 3 mosquitoes.

— *Frank Thomas, NY Mets baseball player, playing in the Houston Astrodome*

In Miami, there are three ways of paying for things: cash, credit card, or stick 'em up.

> — *Pat Williams, knocking Miami, and hoping*
> *to establish an NBA team in Orlando, Florida*

Florida is for old people and their parents.

> — *Harry Dalton, Milwaukee Brewers general manager,*
> *on why he enjoys Arizona for spring training*

I told the players I'd give a bonus to anyone who stays out late tonight.

> — *Billy Martin, on the lack of excitement*
> *in Punta Gorda, Florida*

My last speech was reviewed in Field & Stream.

> — *George Raveling, Washington State basketball coach,*
> *on the remoteness of the school*

I was real sorry to leave Green Bay—for about 10 seconds.

> — *Elijah Pitts, pro football player,*
> *on being traded from Green Bay to Chicago*

I like the folks up there. They walk just the way I do.

> — *Floyd Little, a bow-legged pro running back,*
> *after his trip to Wyoming*

The old neighborhood was so tough they raffled off 2 cars with the cops still in them.

> — *Frank Lucchesi, Philadelphia Phillies manager,*
> *on the old location of the ball park*

Basketball is a religion here. When they get divorces here they don't care about alimony, just who gets the tickets.

> — *Eddie Sutton, Kentucky basketball coach*

It's so small we don't even have a town drunk, everyone has to take a turn.

> — *Stan Hack, baseball player,*
> *on his home town, Grand Tour, IL*

We practice with one nostril taped up. Then we ask Larry Philpot to smoke a cigar on the bus.

— Bob Dinaberg, California Western football coach, on preparing for the smog in Los Angeles

There is nothing worse than being all dressed up with no place to go.

— Walt Frazier, basketball player, after being traded from the NY Knicks to the Cleveland Cavaliers

I do a lot of the same things, I just don't do them outdoors.

— Bill Walton, Boston Celtics basketball player, on settling on the East Coast

I hate playing in the Astrodome. You can't dig in. You can't spit. You remember you're inside on a rug so you don't allow yourself to spit.

— Tom Day, Buffalo Bills football player

I'd rather be in jail in Sacramento than live in Boston.

— Bill Russell, Sacramento Kings coach

I must have. I remember the bar across the street.

— Rod Laver, when asked if he had ever played in a tournament in Orange, New Jersey

The only difference between Candlestick Park and San Quentin is that at Candlestick they let you go home at night.

— Jim Wohlford, outfielder

You should get caught doing something bad, like throwing bombs at archdukes, for them to put you there.

— Bob Knepper, pitcher, on Candlestick Park

It used to be about 125 population, but now it's just a country town.

— Yancy Dounds, Texas A & M guard, on his town, Deadwood, Texas

Only a place that calls an earthquake a fire could call Candlestick a ballpark.

— *Jim Murray, Los Angeles Times columnist*

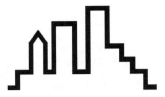

What do you expect? They boo their own fans here. The left-field bleacher fans boo the right field, the right field boos home plate.

— *Dave Johnson, NY Mets manager,*
on Wrigley Field fans

I looked it up, and December 21 is the shortest day of the year. So that's when I'm going to do it.

— *Charles Luken, Cincinnati mayor, fulfilling a bet*
to deliver chili to the mayor of Cleveland

I've seen better ice on the roads in Saskatchewan.

— *Emile Francis, New York Rangers coach,*
on the ice in Madison Square Garden

A word about Florida. It's as flat as a barber shop quartet after midnight. It's surrounded by salt water and covered by fresh air. It's a great place if you're a mosquito. An old mosquito.

— *Jim Murray, The Best of Jim Murray*

I enjoyed my stay in Cleveland. It was nice in Washington, but I'm really looking forward to Seattle.

— *Tim McCormick, drafted in the NBA by Cleveland,*
quickly traded to Washington,
and traded to Seattle a moment later

I'd rather lose and live in Provo than win and live in Laramie.

— *Lavell Edwards, Brigham Young football coach,*
after losing to Wyoming in a severe snowstorm

Four feet away from the moose's butt.

— *Chico Resch, New Jersey Devils,*
on where Moosejaw, Saskatchewan is near

It was strange. The only English words I saw were Sony and Mitsubishi.

> — *Bill Gullickson, ex-major leaguer, now playing in Japan*

It's so cold out there I saw a dog chasing a cat and they were both walking.

> — *Mickey Rivers, Texas Rangers, playing on a cold, windy day*

It was so small, that when I stuck the key in the lock I broke the window.

> — *Tom McVie, Maine Mariners, American Hockey League, on his hotel room*

I only want to check out. I don't want to buy no hotel.

> — *Moses Malone, basketball star, looking at his hotel bill*

If summer falls on a Sunday, they have a picnic.

> — *John Mooney, Salt Lake City Tribune sports editor, on the short summers in Wyoming*

Right now I've eliminated Teheran and Three Mile Island.

> — *Bill Walton, on what city would he choose if he became a free agent*

It's a very small town. It's so small, in fact, that the #1 industry there is taking bottles back to the store.

> — *Monte Clark, San Francisco 49ers coach, on his hometown, Kingsburg*

I'm from New York. Other than riding those subways at night, do New Yorkers ever get nervous?

> — *Lloyd Free, at an NBA playoff game, if he was nervous*

I put my suitcase down, looked up at the Sears Tower, and said "Chicago, I'm going to conquer you." Then I looked down and my suitcase was gone.

> — *James (Quick) Tillis, boxer, when he came to Chicago*

This is nice. What would it take to dome the whole province?

> — *Ken Singleton, Montreal Expos broadcaster,*
> *on the new dome at Olympic Stadium*

I wouldn't say it's cold, but every year, Winnipeg's athlete of the year is an ice fisherman.

> — *Dale Tallon, Chicago Blackhawks announcer,*
> *on a game in Winnipeg*

Chicago is the city of broad shoulders and narrow trophy cases.

> — *Bob Verdi, Chicago Tribune*

Only in Los Angeles do the guys in the radio booth wear make-up.

> — *Gary Park, sportscaster*

They had room at the Los Angeles Coliseum for 93,000 people and two outfielders.

> — *Lindsay Nelson, sportscaster*

My tickets in the Coliseum are seat 67, aisle 72, Highway 99.

> — *Art Linkletter, television personality*

This wouldn't be such a bad place to play if it wasn't for that wind. I guess that's like saying hell wouldn't be such a bad place if it wasn't so hot.

> — *Jerry Reuss, Los Angeles Dodgers pitcher,*
> *on Candlestick Park*

It will revolutionize baseball. It will open a new area of alibis for the players.

> — *Gabe Paul, Cleveland Indians president,*
> *on the Astrodome*

If the Astrodome is the eighth wonder of the world, the rent is the ninth.

> — *Bud Adams, Houston Oilers owner*

RELATIONSHIPS

I got along with Halas just fine. If he'd paid me a little more, I might have even liked him.

> — *Doug Atkus, on his relationship with George Halas*

We have great rapport. He tells me what to do and I do it.

> — *Marvin Barnes, St. Louis Spirits,*
> *on his relationship with his coach*

Bobby Knight could make Switzerland take sides.

> — *Alan Greenberg, Hartford Courant writer*

We have friends just like other people. Of course, you can't fraternize with ballplayers. But who wants to fraternize with ballplayers.

> — *Joe Linsalata, major league umpire*

There has never been any romance between us.

> — *Charles Goren, world master bridge player,*
> *on why he has been able to maintain his partnership*
> *with Mrs. Helen Sobel after more than 20 years*

He's becoming more open. Last time I talked to him he even said three words, "Send me money."

> — *Walt Frazier, pro basketball star,*
> *on the effect of college on his brother, Keith*

I certainly hope so.

> — *Kate Schmidt, Olympic javelin thrower,*
> *if there was any hanky-panky during the Olympics*

PERSONALITIES

I don't have much of a personality. If they paid you on the basis of your personality, I'd make about $2.00 a year.

> — *Mike Ivie, San Francisco Giants infielder*

Over the years, I'd come to understand Al Davis had a personality problem. He didn't have one.

> — *Gene Klein, San Diego Chargers owner,*
> *on his long-time adversary*

A bar in Chicago asked him to leave because they wanted to have Happy Hour.

> — *Bob Player, St. Louis Blues, on Vachov Nedomansky,*
> *who is noted for being gloomy*

It takes 15 muscles to smile and 65 muscles to frown. This leads me to believe Wimp is suffering from muscle fatigue.

> — *Sonny Smith, Auburn basketball coach,*
> *on the disposition of Wimp Sanderson, Alabama coach*

I don't know. I only played there nine years.

> — *Walt Garrison, Dallas Cowboys,*
> *when asked if Tom Landry smiles*

 **M**cEnroe wouldn't be popular if he married Marie Osmond.

> — *Terry Kelleher, writer, when John McEnroe said John*
> *Lloyd was more popular because he was married to*
> *Chris Evert*

Well, there's no question we'll get more mileage out of this than we would with a Bulgarian chemist.

> — *Leo Monahan, University of Massachusetts,*
> *on awarding a doctorate to colorful Red Auerbach*

TALL TALES

He could have hit .300 with a fountain pen.

> — *Joe Garagiola, sportscaster, on Stan Musial*

He could throw a cream puff through a battleship.

> — *Johnny Frederick, Brooklyn Dodger outfielder,*
> *on teammate Dazzy Vance*

Cool Papa Bell was so fast he could get out of bed, turn out the lights across the room, and be back in bed before the lights went out.

> — *Josh Gibson, Negro Leagues catcher*

He once hit a ball between my legs so hard that my center fielder caught it on the fly backing up against the wall.

> — *Dizzy Dean, St. Louis Cardinals pitcher,*
> *on New York Giants infielder Bill Terry*

The neighborhood where I grew up was so tough, the Avon Lady was Sonny Liston.

> — *George Raveling, former Washington*
> *State University basketball coach*

Some day Zahn's going to deliver the ball, and by the time it gets there, he's going to find that the batter's been waived out of the league or been traded.

> — *Bob Lemon, New York Yankees manager,*
> *on slow-pitching Geoff Zahn*

He's got a gun concealed about his person. They can't tell me he throws them balls with his arm.

> — *Ring Lardner, writer, on Washington*
> *Senators pitcher Walter Johnson*

If I'm hitting, I can hit anyone. If not, my twelve-year old son can get me out.

> — *Willie Stargell, Pittsburgh Pirates outfielder*

It actually giggles at you as it goes by.

> — *Rick Monday, Los Angeles Dodgers outfielder,*
> *on Phil Niekro's knuckleball*

Before the All-Star Game he came into the clubhouse and took off his shoes, and they ran another mile without him.

> — *Hank Aaron, Atlanta Braves outfielder, on Pete Rose*

He could get his point if you put him in a tin can and closed the lid.

> — *Mike Newlin, Houston Rockets guard,*
> *on teammate Calvin Murphy*

Sam was born warmed up. If you cut him, Three-in-One oil would come out, not blood.

> — *Gardner Dickinson, professional golfer,*
> *on colleague Sam Snead*

He should be in the Hall of Fame with a tube of K-Y Jelly attached to his plaque.

> — *Gene Mauch, California Angels manager,*
> *on Gaylord Perry's greasing the ball*

Well, I was sitting at a soda fountain one day in a tight-fitting sweater...

> — *Jim Bouton, former major league pitcher,*
> *on how he got into the movies*

TEAMWORK

I played so bad I thought the only way for me to help my team would be to have a heart attack. Then I realized that would be a stroke, too.

> — *Foster Brooke, comedian, on his golf game*

All pitchers are liars and crybabies.

> — *Yogi Berra, New York Yankees catcher*

We're a one-man team, so John Elway has a curfew. The other 44 guys can do what they want.

> — *Dan Reeves, Denver Broncos coach, on team curfews*

Catchers anticipate. They try to receive vibrations, waves. Catchers have to be very sensitive. Their attention wanders a lot. So you have to stop, shake them, get all the screws back in the right place. If my catcher wants to come out to the mound and tell me how bad I am, I'll say, 'You're right, so what shall we do about it?' I give everybody their own space.

> — *Bill Lee, Montreal Expos pitcher,*
> *quoted in* Catcher in the Wry *by Bob Uecker*

Sometimes the first sign a relief pitcher gets from the catcher is to wipe the mustard off his mouth.

> — *Joe Garagiola,* Baseball Is A Funny Game

Pitchers aren't athletes.

> — *Chuck Hiller, New York Mets infielder*

If one of our guys went down, I just doubled it. No confusion there. It didn't require a Rhodes Scholar. If two of my teammates went down, four of yours would. I had to protect my guys.

> — *Don Drysdale, former Los Angeles Dodgers pitcher*

FAMILY MATTERS

I always say that I am going to talk about sex and marriage, but as a football coach's wife, I don't know much about either.

> — *Anne Hayes, wife of football coach Woody Hayes,*
> *speaking to a womens' club*

I understand Doug gave his wife a water bed. She called it the Dead Sea.

> — *Frank Layden, Utah Jazz basketball coach, about*
> *Denver Nuggets coach, Doug Moe*

When I get home, my wife always has my robe, slippers and hot water waiting for me. She hates for me to wash the dishes in cold water.

> — *Duffy Daugherty, Michigan State football coach*

My ex-wives were all good housekeepers. When they left, they kept the house.

> — *Willie Pep, retired featherweight champion,*
> *who had a number of marriages*

What husband isn't.

> — *Anne Hayes, wife of football coach Woody Hayes,*
> *to a heckler who said, "Your husband's a fathead!"*

Divorce, no. Murder, yes.

> — *Anne Hayes, wife of football coach Woody Hayes,*
> *when asked if she felt like divorcing him*

I'm fairly confident that if I died tomorrow, Don would find a way to preserve me until the season was over and he had time for a nice funeral.

> — *Dorothy Shula, wife of Miami Dolphins*
> *football coach Don Shula*

That Knight's a lucky guy. He has a wife who makes a million dollars a year. Mine spends that.

> — *Pete Rose, Cincinnati Reds manager, on Ray Knight, who is married to Nancy Lopez*

If anybody knows a lady doctor. That would make my mother happy.

> — *Sandy Koufax, Los Angeles Dodgers pitcher, unmarried at the time*

My first wife.

> — *Muhammad Ali, heavyweight champion, on his toughest rival*

My 6-foot tall mother.

> — *Brian Uesman, Hope College basketball player, on who affected him the most*

Not if he can swing a golf club.

> — *Joe Montana, San Francisco 49ers quarterback, asked if he would want his son to play football*

He does the same thing when I show him my report card.

> — *Kevin Cassidy, teenage son of Cal State basketball coach, Pete Cassidy, at a game where his father disputed a call by kicking, throwing his arms around, and pacing up and down the court*

The other day I ran out of money, so I asked Coach for $5. He told me I'm a player and the rules don't permit a coach to give money to a player.

> — *Tim Salem, University of Minnesota football team, on his father, Joe, the coach*

Everything went all right until I put the socks in the microwave to dry.

> — *Sammy Stewart, Boston Red Sox, when he watched his kids for a day*

My wife said, "That shouldn't disappoint you. You weren't my first choice, either."

> — *Dave Bliss, accepting the basketball coaching job at New Mexico, after Bobby Knight had been offered the job*

I told them it was the last collect call I'd ever make.

> — *Todd Blackledge, calling his parents, after signing a big contract with the Kansas City Chiefs*

Just financially.

> — *Terry Bradshaw, Pittsburgh Steelers, when asked if he was still involved with Jo Jo Starbuck, his estranged wife*

Next time it'll be different. I think I figured out what I'm doing wrong.

> — *Cale Yorborough, stockcar driver, hoping for a son after his wife gave birth to their second daughter*

These two seats are split by a pole and I could never understand it. Then I found out that this guy was taking his wife to the game. He put her on one side of the pole and he sat on the other.

> — *Vinnie Aleles, NY Yankees season ticket taker, about a regular customer who kept the same 2 seats*

They're married to them.

> — *Forrest Gregg, Cincinnati Bengals football coach, on why he permitted his players to sleep with their wives before a game*

The game was being televised back in Chester, PA, and I wanted my wife and kids to get a look at me.

> — *Danny Murtaugh, Pittsburgh Pirates manager, explaining why, for no apparent reason, he ran out on the baseball field*

I know five reasons why he isn't going to beat me out . . . my wife and four children.

> — *Willie Miranda, baseball player, when he*
> *felt a rookie threatened his regular position*

My wife.

> — *Steve Zegalia, Syracuse football player,*
> *on who he wanted listed as his roommate*

Whoever stole it, is spending less than my wife.

> — *Ilie Nastase, pro tennis player,*
> *on reporting his wallet lost*

Philadelphia at Milwaukee.

> — *Ed Batagowski, NBA referee,*
> *on where his daughter was born*

Sometimes I look on Roy as my nephew, but sometimes only as my sister's son.

> — *Gene Mauch, Minnesota Twins manager, on*
> *having his nephew, Ron Smalley, on the Twins*

Miss Taylor is a beautiful woman, sure. But how do I know she won't nag me. Can she cook? Can she handle money? Can she keep the house neat? Can I talk baseball with her?

> — *Harry Walker, Houston Astros manager,*
> *saying he would not trade his wife for Elizabeth Taylor*

It's a good thing Brian was a third child, or he would have been the only one.

> — *Kathy Bosworth, Brian Bosworth's mother*

Because his mother wants it that way.

> — *Ed Murphy, Mississippi basketball coach,*
> *on why he started center Sean Murphy*

I never realized how short a month is, until I started paying alimony.

> — *Harry Caray, sports announcer*

Because if it didn't work out, I didn't want to blow the whole day.

> — *Paul Hornung, Green Bay Packers,*
> *on why he got married at 11 a.m.*

I'm going to have to buy a tractor to pull the plow.

> — *Raymond Henson, on his son Champ*
> *leaving to play pro football*

My daughter Kelly is five, and is a friend of Ken Boswell's daughter Ashley, who is the same age. They hadn't seen each other for a while, and Ashley asked my wife if Kelly had been traded.

> — *Jerry DaVanon, Houston Astros reserve player*

I have six kids and 100 quarterhorses to feed and I'm not sure which group eats the most.

> — *Gary Player, pro golfer, and rancher*

I was going to wait and get married after we won our first game. But we decided against that.

> — *Dewey Selmon, Tampa Bay Buccaneers,*
> *who lost 26 straight games and then got married*

If I said, "Fall down" he's going to fall down. I'm still his father.

> — *Joe Frazier, fighter, if he faced his*
> *son, Marvis, who is also a fighter*

When my son was a tot he wet the bed. [I told him] "Son, Joe DiMaggio never did anything like that," and he replied, "Oh yeah, well my idol is Pee Wee Reese."

> — *Lefty Gomez*

We went the animal route. It cost more to feed, but not as much to educate them.

> — *Glen Hanlon, Detroit Red Wings,*
> *with no children, but with numerous pets*

All it means is that my wife will get a potted plant instead of a diamond necklace for our anniversary in August.

> — *Bill Laimbeer, Detroit Pistons basketball player,*
> *after being fined $5,000 by the league*

My wife made me a millionaire. I used to have three million.

> — *Bobby Hull, former hockey great, after his divorce*

My wife wanted a big diamond.

> — *Mookie Wilson, NY Mets,*
> *planning to be married in a baseball stadium*

I wouldn't want my daughter to have to deal with this kind of life. For that matter, I don't think it's such a great life for the dog, either.

> — *Mickey Shuler, NY Jets football player,*
> *who was difficult at home*

I didn't hire Scott because he's my son. I hired him because I'm married to his mother.

> — *Frank Layden, Utah Jazz coach, on his assistant coach*

You have to pay for a wife in my country. If you don't have money or a cow, it's hard to get married. I pay 80 cows, 32 so far. I owe some. When I go back home, I pay. In America, all you have to pay for is the party to get married.

> — *Manute Bol, center Golden State Warriors,*
> *on his native Sudan*

Basketball

Basketball can serve as a kind of metaphor for ultimate cooperation. It is a sport where success, as symbolized by the championship, requires that the dictates of community prevail over selfish personal impulses.

> —— *Bill Bradley, New York Knickerbockers*

The basketball is a tool that the black has now, same as maybe once he had a plow.

> — *Willis Reed, New York Knickerbockers*

A black man has to fight for respect in basketball, season after season. And I measure that respect in the figures on my contract.

> — *Kareem Abdul-Jabbar, Los Angeles Lakers*

Playgrounds are the best place to learn the game, because if you lose, you sit down.

> — *Gary Williams, American University basketball coach*

We have a great bunch of outside shooters. Unfortunately, all of our games are played indoors.

> — *Weldon Drew, New Mexico State basketball coach*

Cal passes and passes and then takes the same shot they had 15 minutes ago.

> — *Johnny Green, UCLA basketball player*

When I was young, college basketball was an extension of the college itself. Now it is a piece of some television network.

> — *Pete Newell, Golden State Warriors scout*

Wrapping it Up

UNCONVENTIONAL WISDOM

When I was young and smart, I couldn't understand Casey Stengel. Now that I'm older and dumber, he makes sense to me.

> — *Sandy Koufax, Los Angeles Dodgers pitcher*

If Frank had known he was going to live so long, he would have taken better care of himself.

> — *Pepper Rodgers, on Clemson football*
> *coach Frank Howard*

The uglier a man's legs are the better he plays golf. It's almost a law.

> — *H.G. Wells, writer*

To a pitcher, a base hit is the perfect example of negative feedback.

> — *Steve Hovley, Seattle Pilots outfielder*

If you ain't got a bullpen, you ain't got nuthin'.

> — *Yogi Berra, New York Yankees manager*

I don't like them fellas who drive in two runs and let in three.

> — *Casey Stengel, New York Yankees manager*

Good stockbrokers are a dime a dozen, but good shortstops are hard to find.

> — *Charles O. Finley, Oakland A's owner*

The two most important things in life are good friends and a strong bullpen.

> — *Bob Lemon, New York Yankees manager*

If you act like you know what you're doing, you can do anything you want, except maybe neurosurgery.

> — *John Lowenstein, Baltimore Orioles*

Only three things can happen when you put the ball in the air, and two of them are bad.

> — *Duffy Daugherty, football coach*

There are two things not long for this world: dogs who chase cars and pro golfers who chip for pars.

> — *Lee Trevino, professional golfer*

A cardinal rule for the club breaker is never to break your putter and driver in the same match or you are dead.

> — *Tommy Bolt, How to Keep Your Temper on the Golf Course*

Trade a player a year too early rather than a year too late.

> — *Branch Rickey, Los Angeles Dodgers executive*

We arrive early, which is good. If you get to the bowl site early, the players go after the girls right away and spend all their money. After that they have to stay in their hotel rooms and concentrate on football.

> — *Don James, University of Washington football coach*

A man's gotta make at least one bet every day, else he could be walking around lucky and never know it.

> — *Jimmy Jones, horse trainer*

It's those rocks they took off the moon. They've got to put them back. Nothing, including the weather, has been the same since.

> — *Rick Camp, Atlanta Braves, after a fight on the field between two players*

If size meant anything, a cow would beat a rabbit.

> — *Herb Stevens, horse trainer, when told one of his horses was too small to win the Kentucky Derby*

Our fielders have to catch a lot of balls, or at least deflect them to someone who can.

> — *Dan Quisenberry, Kansas City Royals*

I'm curious about jumping off a cliff and I don't do that either.

> — *Herschel Walker, Dallas Cowboys,*
> *on why he wasn't even "curious" about taking a drink*

I like steak and good food like that, but mostly steak. If you eat hot dogs, you play like one. If you eat hamburgers, you play like one...flat.

> — *Chuck Thorpe, golf pro*

All the time it's fasten your goddamn seat belt. But how come every time I read about one of those plane crashes, there's 180 people on board and all 180 die? Didn't any of them have their seat belt fastened?

> — *Fred Talbot, Seattle Pilots pitcher*

You either have to finesse 12 people who aren't smart enough to get out of jury duty, or 11 who aren't smart enough to play offense.

> — *Steve Fuller, Clemson quarterback,*
> *on choosing between law or pro football*

Playing on the road is only an advantage if you win. If you lose, you're better off playing on the road, because you have a better chance of getting out of the stadium alive.

> — *Lou Holtz, University of Arkansas football coach*

PHILOSOPHY

Everybody wants to go to heaven, but nobody wants to die.

> — *Joe Louis, ex-heavyweight champion*

Some days you tame the tiger, and some days the tiger has you for lunch.

> — *Tug McGraw, Philadelphia Phillies relief pitcher*

The owners think if I wasn't in baseball I'd be out digging ditches or something. That really fries me. How can they be in baseball and not see what it's all about? Pitching is a beautiful thing. It's an art.

> — *Tom Seaver, New York Mets pitcher*

The pitcher is the happiest with his arm idle. He prefers to dawdle in the present, knowing that as soon as he gets on the mound and starts his windup he delivers himself to the uncertainty of the future.

> — *George Plimpton,* Out of My League

Has anyone ever satisfactorily explained why the bad hop is always the last one?

> — *Hank Greenwald, sportscaster*

If this is the ultimate game, how come they're gonna play it again next year?

> — *Duane Thomas, Dallas Cowboys running back, on the Super Bowl*

The way I look at it, a home run is just a fly ball that goes a little farther.

> — *Ron Darling, New York Mets pitcher*

It's like climbing the highest mountain and finding that the guru at the top doesn't know the meaning of life.

> — *Ken Plutnicki, Harvard basketball team, after a narrow loss to a heavily-favored team*

To err is human, to forgive divine. I forgot who said it, but I think it was Joey Amalfitano.

> — *Tommy Lasorda*

If "ifs" were gifts, every day would be Christmas.

> — *Charles Barkley, Philadelphia 76ers*

Luck is what you have left over after you give 100%.

> — *Langston Coleman, Nebraska end*

Never let hope elude you. That is life's biggest fumble.

> — *Bob Zuppke, football coach*

I like to ride bicycles, walk in the woods, just walk around, sit on the curb. Like the old Greeks. I want to contemplate life. Let the women do the work.

> — *Luther Lassiter, champion pocket billiards player, claiming he hasn't worked since he was 15*

There's nothing in the world I wouldn't do for Walter O'Malley. There's nothing he wouldn't do for me. That's the way we go through life, doing nothing for each other.

> — *Gene Autry, California Angels owner*

They say the breaks all even up in the long run, but how many of us last that long?

> — *Chuck Knox, Seattle Seahawks football coach*

Philosophy is just a hobby. You can't open up a philosophy factory.

> — *Dewey Selmon, Tampa Bay Buccaneers, on earning a Ph.D. in philosophy*

Life is but a game of football.

> — *Sir Walter Scott, English poet*

SIMPLE TRUTHS

Potential is a French word that means you aren't worth a damn yet.

> — *Jeff Van Note, Atlanta Falcons,*
> *on some potential players*

They let you chase girls, they just don't let you catch them.

> — *Glen Kozlowski, Brigham Young University,*
> *on the power of the Mormon Church*

The reason I don't have a curfew is because it's always our star who gets caught.

> — *Abe Lemons, Oklahoma City basketball coach*

You don't spit into the wind, you don't tug on Superman's cape and you don't mess with star football players.

> — *Marianne Jennings, Arizona State faculty*
> *representative, resigning because she was*
> *overruled on a star football player's eligibility*

I thought all you had to be was good enough.

> — *Brian Piccolo, Wake Forest's leading college rusher,*
> *when told he probably would be too slow and too short*
> *to play in the NFL*

In baseball, when a player scores, you cheer. In football, when a player scores, you look for flags.

> — *Thomas Boswell, Washington Post columnist*

A pitcher who walks Babe Ruth throws a party. A pitcher who walks Freddie Patek wants to go home and kick the dog.

> — *Whitey Herzog, Kansas City Royals baseball*
> *manager*

It would be nice to coach a team like that, but I'd rather own it.

> — *Bobby Orr, hockey player, if he would like to coach a team with both Gordie Howe and Bobby Hull*

I personally have taken the approach that if you can't win the first one, you can't possibly have an undefeated season.

> — *Charlie Coffey, Arkansas football coach*

That's because he was born before I was.

> — *Johnny Unitas, on George Blanda being older than him*

It hurts knowing that they can do without you. I was always led to believe that I was indispensable.

> — *Greg Pruitt, Oklahoma star player, after they beat Nebraska, while he sat on the bench because of injuries*

If you hang in there long enough and grit your teeth hard enough, your orthodontist bill will go up.

> — *Stan Morrison, college basketball coach*

I looked in my glove and then on the ground. That left only one place...the other side of the fence.

> — *Pat Kelly, Baltimore Orioles outfielder, after a home run*

There are two things I've never heard. I've never heard my daddy cuss, and I never heard of a school on probation say they got justice.

> — *Darrell Royal, Texas athletic director*

I play as well on the road as I do at home, but my teams don't.

> — *Lou Holtz, Arkansas football coach, commenting on road games*

CONVENTIONAL WISDOM

You just have to treat death like any other part of life.
> — *Tom Sneva, Indy race car driver*

Sweat plus sacrifice equals success.
> — *Charles O. Finley, Oakland A's owner*

Luck is the residue of design.
> — *Branch Rickey, St. Louis Cardinals general manager*

If you think long, you think wrong.
> — *Jim Kaat, Minnesota Twins pitcher*

The future is now.
> — *George Allen, Washington Redskins coach*

It's what you learn, after you know it all, that counts.
> — *John Wooden, UCLA basketball coach*

Do for yourself or do without.
> — *Gaylord Perry, Cleveland Indians pitcher*

Everywhere, I hear the Boston Celtics are having trouble. I think if you live in Afghanistan, that's having trouble.
> — *Frank Layden, Utah Jazz coach,*
> *after his team was beaten by the Celtics*

If you make every game a life-and-death situation, you're going to have problems. For one thing, you'll be dead a lot.
> — *Dean Smith, North Carolina basketball coach*

I NSPIRATION

Go out that door to victory.

> — *Knute Rockne, University of Notre Dame*
> *football coach, after an inspiring half-time talk*

Don't let failure get you down. Babe Ruth struck out over 1,300 times.

> — *Lou Holtz, Notre Dame football coach*

Sometime, Rock, when the team's up against it, when things are wrong and the breaks are beating the boys, ask them to win one for the Gipper. I don't know where I'll be then, Rock, but I'll know about it and I'll be happy.

> — *George Gipp, Notre Dame halfback,*
> *from his deathbed speech to coach Knute Rockne*

A head coach is guided by one primary objective-to dig, claw, wheedle, coax that fanatical effort out of his players. He wants his team to play on Saturday, as if they were planting the flag on Iwo Jima.

> *Darrell Royal, Texas football coach*

The Last Hurrahs
(As Time Goes By)

RETIREMENT

I eat less, weigh less, train less and care less.
> — *Ray "Boom Boom" Mancini,*
> *after he had stopped fighting*

Anything where I don't have to do anything...like a politician maybe.
> — *Louis Lipps, Pittsburgh Steelers,*
> *on his retirement plans*

I ain't doing a damn thing, and I don't start until noon.
> — *Bum Phillips, retired football coach*

Not for a million dollars. No, I have to take that back.
> — *Red Kelly, retired hockey star,*
> *if he would come out of retirement*

All that's happening to me is that my self-winding watch has run down.
> — *Weeb Ewbank, retired NY Jets coach*

I can say now that I'll know when I want to get out, but when I reach that time, I may not know.
> — *Jack Nicklaus, talking about retirement*

Retire? Retire to what? I already fish and play golf.
> — *Julius Boros, pro golfer, on retirement*

I'd like to be an entrepreneur. They threw the word about in economics and I always wondered what it meant.
> — *Bert Jones, Baltimore Colts quarterback,*
> *on his future*

GROWING OLD

For aging boxers, first your legs go, then your reflexes go, then your friends go.

> — *Willie Pep, former featherweight champion*

How could he call me old?

> — *Buddy Ryan, Eagles coach, when Steve Ossie said, "That's the ramblings of a pathetic, senile, old man."*

You lose an awful lot of speed between 80 and 86.

> — *Ruth Rothfarb, 86-year old marathon runner, on why she didn't think she could beat her own marathon time*

When you win, you're an old pro. When you lose, you're an old man.

> — *Charlie Connerly, New York Giants quarterback*

Middle age is when you start for home about the same time you used to start for somewhere else.

> — *Chris Dundee, fight promoter*

Once a pitcher loses his fastball, he has to go to garbage.

> — *Jim O'Toole, retired Cincinnati Reds pitcher, now working for a waste-disposal company*

The older you get, the longer you used to be.

> — *Chi Chi Rodriguez, professional golfer*

When I caught the ball, it was a bright, sunny day. By the time I got to the end zone, it was partly cloudy.

> — *George Martin, NY Giants defensive lineman, on his slowing down*

The new players keep getting better, and it makes you think you're getting worse.

> — *Alex Sandusky, veteran Baltimore*
> *Colts offensive guard*

One day headlines, the next day breadlines.

> — *Lenny Mancini, former boxer*

As men grow older, the toys get more expensive.

> — *Marvin Davis, on purchasing*
> *the Oakland A's for many millions*

There's a conspiracy among the clubs. Nobody's hiring 37-year old players who can't hit.

> — *Mike Jorgensen, ex-baseball player*

Stay busy, get plenty of exercise and don't drink too much. Then again, don't drink too little.

> — *Herman Smith-Johannsen, 103-year old*
> *Canadian cross-country skier, on his long life*

I knew it was time to quit when I was chewing out an official and he walked off the penalty faster than I could keep up with him.

> — *George Halas, retired Chicago Bears football coach*

There ought to be a rule that when the temperature drops below your age you don't have to play.

> — *Graig Nettles, Atlanta Braves baseball player*

Oldtimers weekends and airplane landings are alike. If you can walk away from them, they're successful.

> — *Casey Stengel, at an Oldtimers Day*

You can have money stacked up to the ceiling, but the size of your funeral is still going to depend on the weather.

> — *Chuck Tanner, Pittsburgh Pirates manager*

I can't run my fingers through my hair.

> — *Kareem Abdul-Jabbar, if there was anything*
> *he couldn't do after his long NBA career*

After 12 years, the old butterflies come back. Well, I guess at my age you call them moths.

> — *Franco Harris, in his first game,*
> *after being traded from Pittsburgh to Seattle*

I have no complaints. If I hadn't made it to 33, then I'd have a complaint.

> — *Jimmy Connors, on reaching 33*

The other day I got a call from Hollywood saying they wanted to do my life story. The only discouraging thing was that Walter Brennan was to play my part.

> — *George Blanda, Oakland Raiders quarterback*

You're too old when it takes you longer to rest up than it does to get tired.

> — *Phog Allen, retired Kansas*
> *basketball coach, on getting old*

I used to pitch, play golf, have fun, rest and pitch again. Now I pitch, recover, recover, recover, rest and pitch again.

> — *Don Sutton, veteran pitcher,*
> *on the process of aging*

I'm like a '67 Cadillac. I've changed the engine twice, rolled back the odometer and replaced the transmission. But now all the tires are goin' flat. It's time to put it in the junkyard.

> — *Lee Trevino, professional golfer*

Index